ΛΡΩCΛLΨPSΣ

THE REVELATION OF JESUS CHRIST

DR. ANA MÉNDEZ FERRELL

Ana Méndez Ferrell Inc.

THANKSGIVING AND DEDICATION

I want to thank my heavily Father, Jesus Christ and the Holy Spirit for giving me the privilege to receive the revelations of this book.

It is to my God in His three persons that I also dedicate this work.

PRAYER

I pray that the eyes of the understanding will be open in every person that reads this book and that they can glorify and know Jesus the Messiah in the revelation of His kingdom.

Ana Méndez Ferrell Inc.

ΛΡΩCΛLΨPSΣ, *The Revelation of Jesus Christ.*

© Dr. Ana Méndez Ferrell

1ST Edition 2012.

All Scripture quotations, unless otherwise indicated, have been taken from the New King James Version and others.

Category: Reformation

Published by: Ana Méndez Ferrell, Inc.
                 P. O. Box 141
                 Ponte Vedra, Florida, 32004-0141
                 United States of America

Printed in: United States of America

www.AnaMendezFerrell.com

ISBN 10: 1-933163-70-4
ISBN 13: 978-1-933163-70-3

CONTENT

FOREWORD

Dr. Rony Chaves

I n my thirty five years of ministry unto the Lord, many dear ministers having right testimonies, have asked me to write a foreword to one of their books or a commentary of the same. They never asked me to such a thing because they thought I was in full agreement with what they wrote but because they thought my years of service unto The Almighty God had given me the maturity, the honesty and the authority to suggest any changes to the subject matter; to freely write about the book and to be able to evaluate in honesty the material regarding the subjects the authors had dealt with.

Along all these years in ministry, my friend's petitions have not only spiritually enriched me by reading and analyzing their material but it has also helped me re-evaluate my own teachings and concepts, whether to revise them in humility or to reinforce them when I did not accept the author's posture.

When I recommend a book such as this one, I don't necessarily do it because I agree with everything written in it but because I consider how important it is to study this subject matter in depth whether to reconsider the eschatological and Kingdom concepts so necessary to be preached nowadays, or to reaffirm what each one thinks, even though it may differ from the approach of the one writing it.

The subject matter in Dr. Ana Mendez's new book will not leave us without reconsidering our own beliefs about the 'the end times." We will have to study, pray and undergo much discussion. It will make us think, analyze, read and research: where do all these things we have believed and supported all these years regarding this subject matter originate from. I am sure that after this exhaustive analysis, we will be all enriched and fortified to apostolically continue edifying the Church and continue working with added strength for the establishment of the Kingdom of God in the nations of the Earth.

COMMENTARY

TIME FOR APOSTOLIC RE-CONSIDERATION:

"In Pursuit of A New Reformation"

Apostle Fernado Orihuela

 reform-pursuing Church needs to revise "what they believe", and the "why" they believe "what" they say "they believe".

Throughout the Church's history, there undoubtedly have been times where certain doctrinal points are considered "untouchable" and beyond all judgment or discussion. The first brethren were divided regarding the baptism of the Holy Spirit upon the Gentiles. The majority of them - and this thanks to the Jerusalem brethren- thought that the Greeks, Romans, and the rest of the converts from the Mediterranean and Asia could not be filled with this wonderful blessing. Joined to this thought was the fact that the concept about non-Jews who had professed their faith in Christ, had to be circumcised and even follow some of the Jewish regulations inherent in the Law, and the Old Covenant.

It was in the community of Antioch - the nucleus of the pioneer church- where the Jewish believers in Jesus had arrived and were shocked to see how the converted members had not been circumcised nor were they complying with other legal Jewish precepts. This is the reason the disciples in that city charged Paul and Barnabas along with "certain other of them " to go to Jerusalem to solve this situation once and for all.

It was at the Jerusalem Council where this matter was dealt with, along other faith points. This gave rise to the first regulatory meeting of the primitive church (towards the year 50 AD) according to the writings in Chapter 15 of the Book of Acts of the Apostles.

Their across-the-board resolution encompassed all groups of believers. "For it seemed good to the Holy Ghost, and to us, to lay upon you no greater burden than these necessary things: that ye abstain from meats offered to idols, and from blood, and from things strangled, and from fornication. If ye keep yourselves from these things, ye shall do well. Fare ye well!" Acts 15:28-29

Defining the issues in a conflict has not always been this easy, the controversy John Wesley had with the Church of England regarding the Baptism of the Holy Spirit and the instantaneous sanctification in the mid-1700's is well known. Undoubtedly, no conciliation was ever reached and the break-up between both positions was the conclusion as had been anticipated by the thinkers of the epoch. The Methodist Church was born as the fruit of this crisis, separated from the Anglican Church to the present day. Nowadays, the Church enjoys benefits not possessed barely two hundred years ago. Towards the end of 1700, thousands of children roamed the streets of Gloucester, England, hungry, dirty and without any schooling. The end of the Victorian Era left such a large amount of unemployed people that entire families had to go out and get a job to enable them to survive. In was in the midst of this situation when in 1785 Robert Raikes began to gather the children who roamed without a destination on Sundays after the workweek.

His objective was to utilize the Gospel as a tool for teaching and for life improvement. For more than twenty-five years he raised "Sunday Schools" forming children with better life aspirations and who could know Jesus Christ as their Savior. Curiously enough, it was the Church itself, who tenaciously opposed this mission. Such a great persecution rose up against Raike's ministry, which was still in developmental stage, to the extent that a law forbidding the existence of "Sunday School", was being sought out to be approved in the English Parliament.

In less than the 50 years following, there were already hundreds of churches using the model created by Raikes who had reached more than 400,000 children. Nowadays, more than two hundred years later, nobody doubts that this is an effective work-tool in the modern church. Its onset was simply not effortless.

One of the most delicate points of the conflict to date is unquestionably Biblical Eschatology. I believe with full certainty that there is currently no other doctrinal matter having a greater number of thorny edges and varying positions. What very few believing people know is that this subject matter was not always the object of so much controversy.

The first reason I support the material written by prophetess Ana Mendez Ferrell is because, regardless whether her conclusions are right or wrong, she has dared to put on the discussion table one of the most respected "sacred cows" of the evangelical tradition.

The second, is because the church that is pursuing a reformation needs to revisit "what it believes", and the "why" it believes "what" it says it believes. The Book of Revelation is one of the least comprehended by modern day church and we need a new exegesis on this precious material.

The third reason is because I know the author up-close and I know she only does that which she has an absolute conviction God is telling her to do and uniquely because of this, am I led to respect her work and seriously consider it, seeking to find the revelation that perhaps for any given reason, we have not previously seen.

I am certain that if we approach this material with humility and with an openness of spirit, God will speak to us. It may not finish clearing up all the doctrinal voids about future events but it shall undoubtedly provoke some reflection, that under all points of view considered, the Church requires now more than ever.

COMMENTARY

Prophet Kevin Leal

Σ lisha stood on the banks of the River Jordan with the mantle of his mentor in his hands, his memory fresh with the power he had just seen with his own eyes. He boldly exercises his faith in the God of his mentor.

"Where is the God of Elijah? He asked, fully expecting the legacy of his mentor to continue with him.

Nothing is harder to do than trying to explain the reality of a Kingdom experience someone else has not had. Even for the best of us, tradition and the status quo often blind us to current Kingdom realities.

In her latest book, Ana Mendez Ferrell points us to the reality that Kingdom Living is not just in the future it is for right now.

The expression of the Kingdom in the Gospels and in the Book of Acts show us the obvious disconnects between what was considered "Kingdom normal" then, and "Kingdom normal" now.

I pray you read this book with fresh eyes.

SECTION I

THE *BOOK OF REVELATION* SEEN FROM THE PROPHETIC PERSPECTIVE OF THE KINGDOM OF GOD

T o interpret the Apocalypse, also known as *Book of Revelation,* has been one of the greatest challenges of all times theologians have faced; if we attempt to analyze it through symbols and precise facts, we will necessarily enter the arena of speculation.

The book you are about to read is unlike anything else written regarding this precious prophetic document John left behind.

My intention is to extract the spiritual truths that will lead us to lay hold of the blessings promised to those who read it and keep its commandments.

This is a key season to understand the Apocalypse, *Book of Revelation* and God is loudly sounding off His trumpet from the heavens announcing the time to talk has arrived.

I write as a prophetess of God with the understanding that we know in part and we prophesy in part. It is not my intention to have the final word in this matter but to shed a new and different light from Heaven so you may see the **Book of Revelation** with new eyes.

In 1999 God took me to the Island of *Patmos,* where John wrote the **Book of Revelation.** During four entire days I was caught up inside the heart of the Father to see and to understand many things that He wants us to understand today.

In that dimension things are seen differently, because this is the realm where **"He is."** So in this study I am not analyzing the *Book of Revelation* sentence by sentence, but I instead I want to share with you, from the Kingdom of God perspective, the greater subjects that compose this prophecy. As we understand them, they will give us light to interpret the whole book.

As you go on reading this book, it is possible that you find things that you don't agree at the first sight. Bear with me and have patience with me. I will built upon each subject, and your understanding will open up in a wider way. There are things you will read that will challenge you, others that are going to provoke you to go deep with God, praying and inquireing. You will find concepts that will totally change the way you think about end time prophecy.

I also understand that there will be things in which your way of thinking is different from mine, and that's fine, too. But what I am completely sure about is that you will never be the same, nor will you conceive of the Kingdom of God the same way as you did when you finish reading this book.

Your Chrsitianity will become wonderful, and you will know God as never before.

1 My Experience In Patmos

I t was September 1999 when I arrived on the island of Patmos. God instructed me to go by myself. He had a plan and an encounter with me that would change my life forever.

The island had remained almost virgin. The port of *Skala* welcomes the tourists, but apart from this quaint little city, one can only find little fishing villages here and there. Also, atop a mountain are found the ruins of an ancient temple of Apollo and a rural road that connects everything in the island.

Since the moment of my arrival, I immediately felt the presence of God as it would have been in the time of John. It was as if time had stopped. By the sea there is a small house that the natives have preserved, and they say it was the place where the beloved disciple used to live. Next to it there is a big stone from where they say he baptized the people who dwelt on the island.

Even though John was sent as a prisoner to *Patmos*, a small population of worshipers of Diana and Apollo also inhabited the island. The island was spiritually ruled by a witch doctor called Kynops who had everybody bewitched with his great wonders. The arrival of the Gospel of the Kingdom produced a major confrontation against the powers of the *queen of heaven* and *witchcraft,* which ended in an event that marked the history of the island. It was an encounter like the one at *Mount Carmel* where Elijah faced the priests of Baal. Here is the account told by Prochorus, John's disciple:

"The sorcerer, full of pride, ridiculed St. John, who simply said, *'his power will come to an end.'* When the crowd heard this, they beat John down and mistreated him leaving him for dead. *'Retire now,'* Kynops said to the people; *'this night the dogs and eagles will devour his corpse.'* Prochorus, weeping, removed his master's body.

Suddenly at two o'clock in the morning he heard from his master's lips these words:
'Prochorus, my son.'
'Why, are you living, my father?'
'Yes go and tell Myron that I am breathing still.'

Prochorus went to find Myron[1] , and in giving him these tidings, both his and his family's grief turned into joy. They hastened to the spot where John was, and found him praying with his head bent towards the East.

Together, they all thanked God for His deliverance.

When Kynops heard the following day that John was still alive, he gave orders to bring him before him and show him his power

---

[1] Myron, another of John's disciples in the island

20

and do greater marvels still than those he had done the day before. The apostle was brought to the same place as the previous day. The crowd again assembled. *'Watch me,'* Kynops said to John, and he plunged into the bay. At this moment the apostle knelt down and prayed to God, and the people heard a great noise in the waters. The crowd, thinking Kynops was returning, waited and watched until they grew tired; but the waves calmed again and Kynops never again returned...thus ends Prochorus's story of Kynops."[2]

After this amazing event, the inhabitants of Patmos received the Gospel and were baptized, a mosaic painting was made to commemorate this historical event.

Depiction of John, the Apostle, defeating the sorcerer Kynops in Patmos.

---

[2] *The Island called Patmos pg 147, William Edgar Geil*

From the moment of my arrival on the island, I had the impression that time had stopped. There was something in the air that merged with an Eternal dimension where time does not exist. I settled in at an inexpensive but comfortable boarding house and rented a motor scooter to transport myself to wherever the Holy Spirit directed me.

The first day I went to the cave where John had received the prophecies contained in the **Book of Revelation.** It's found in the midst of a beautiful wild forest halfway up the mountain on one of the three volcanoes that form the island. Right before the cave's entrance, there is a flat large stone engraved with the scripture of Revelation 1:

I was in the Spirit on the Lord's Day, and I heard behind me a loud voice, as of a trumpet, saying, "I am the Alpha and the Omega, the First and the Last," and, "What you see, write in a book and send it to the seven churches which are in Asia: to Ephesus, to Smyrna, to Pergamos, to Thyatira, to Sardis, to Philadelphia, and to Laodicea." Then I turned to see the voice that spoke with me. And having turned I saw seven golden lampstands, and in the midst of the seven lampstands One like the Son of Man, clothed with a garment down to the feet and girded about the chest with a golden band. His head and hair were white like wool, as white as snow, and His eyes like a flame of fire; His feet were like fine brass, as if refined in a furnace, and His voice as the sound of many waters; He had in His right hand seven stars, out of His mouth went a sharp two-edged sword, and His countenance was like the sun shining in its strength.

And when I saw Him, I fell at His feet as dead. But He laid His right hand on me, saying to me, "Do not be afraid; I am the First and the Last. I am He who lives, and was dead, and behold, I am alive forevermore. Amen. And I have the keys of Hades and of Death."

Revelation 1:9-18

While I was reading this, the Holy Spirit came upon me and my eyes began watering and my body began shaking. I was standing in the very place where Jesus became manifest in His glory, and His presence was still there. I walked slowly to the cave with great expectation in my heart and found nobody there, as if the Lord had prepared it just for me.

Despite how the Greek Orthodox had defiled the cave with icons, the Presence of God was so strong that the painted images seemed like smoke having no power.

I remained there for awhile and then walked out to the forest where the hand of man had not yet destroyed the beauty of the place. I sat under the trees and entered into the Spirit as I worshipped the Lord. Little by little the atmosphere became charged with an intense presence of angels and then before my open eyes I saw the door in Heaven, the same that John saw in the first century.

It appeared with a deep blue color in the midst of the clear summer sky. Heavenly light shimmered around its edges. I was paralyzed in a state of ecstasy when as clear as one can hear on Earth, I heard the trumpet voice of God saying, "Come up here!"

At once, the Spirit caught me up as with an invisible gigantic hand, and I appeared 2,000 years ago on *Mount Calvary,* at the very moment of Christ's crucifixion. But there was something very strange for me to comprehend; it was as if the apostle John and I were the same person. I saw my body and it was John's; my emotions and thoughts were no longer mine, but his. I was feeling exactly what he felt when he was seeing his Beloved hanging on the cross.

My heart was destroyed with grief, or his, I don't know; we were one and the same.

As I watched Jesus hanging from the cross, all of his wounds made my own body ache. I saw his bruised deformed face, and I wanted to throw myself upon Him and clean, with kisses of love, the blood that ran down His cheeks. He looked into my eyes. His eyes were almost swollen shut and glassy with the look of death beginning to invade them. Even so, He looked at me and filled me with His love.

From His eyes flowed silent words that said to me, "Thank you for being with Me in My pain. Thank you for not leaving Me alone. The Father and the Spirit have distanced Themselves because of the sin that is upon Me. Your love gives Me strength, beloved. Stay with Me until the end."

"Yes! Yes!" my heart shouted, or John's heart. I don't know, it was like being blended together with him.

Suddenly, the body of the Lord began to tremble, and a deep, distressed cry left his lips. I felt it pierce me. *"My beloved, my beloved!*

24

Don't go!" shouted my soul, as the cry of His death resonated within me like a deafening bell. It had been imprinted on my soul, and I could not stop hearing it. The earth began to shake, and the heavens darkened. There was confusion everywhere. Shouts were heard. I was paralyzed, like John. I was living everything that John felt. My eyes were fixed upon Jesus. I could not believe that my beloved was there…dead.

The sound of the Roman army's armor brought me back to my senses. With violence and without any mercy whatsoever, they approached the two hung thieves, and broke their legs, but when they came to Jesus, since they saw that He was already dead, they stopped. One of the soldiers kept looking at me with disgust, and then he turned away. With his spear, he pierced the heart of my beloved. Right there in front of me, I saw Jesus' heart open and blood and water come out of his side. *"I, John, am the one giving testimony of this."*

While I looked at the wound in His side, the heart of Jesus changed into the heart of the Father. Suddenly, I saw, as it were, a door that opened inside this great vital organ, and the Spirit took me inside. Inside was like the tabernacle, having walls of flesh. There was the Courtyard, the Holy Place, and the Holy of Holies. I spent four whole days there. Each part of this impressive place was full of wounds and open lacerations. They were different and of differing severity. These are the marks of pain that remain recorded in the heart of the Father due to sin. Sin tears His insides apart in a very painful way. Inside, there were sins that affected the Courtyard, others the Holy Place, and others, where I saw the most serious wounds, went all the way into the Holy of Holies.

During the days I spent there, the Lord spoke to me about each one of His wounds. I spent a lot of time in the Holy of Holies. The pain there was the most intense. I asked the Holy Spirit what these wounds were, what kinds of sins were so horrible that they caused this depth of damage inside the Father's heart? He told me, *"These are the sins against love in any of its forms: divisions, hatred among the brethren, slander, treason, criticism, when they attack and destroy each other, when they persecute one another filled with jealousy, when they annihilate the fallen and they hate amongst themselves. These are the sins that wound the Father the most,"* He added.

Then God showed me the impressive holiness of love. God is love, and His love shines with a dazzling brilliance because it is Holy. This Holiness emanates from His own heart and is, in itself, the Holy of Holies. It was an extremely reverential glory before me while His love surrounded and consumed me like an intensely powerful fire that filled me in a gigantic wave of life, of grace, and of mercy. It was impressively pure and holy- infinitely HOLY. It was the heart of God.

As a truth impressed upon my spirit, the Lord spoke to me about the Holy of Holies of His own heart. This is the place of complete, full fellowship of deepest intimacy between God and man. It is where the fullness designed to fill our hearts finds it highest manifestation. It is there that our heart finds total and perfect union with God. It is where the Spirit of God joins with our spirit to become ONE with Him.

Then I heard a voice that came forth from the midst of the glorious holiness, and it said to me, **"My love is holy, and there is no possibility of holiness outside of My love."**

Holiness has nothing to do with religious conduct. It is a matter of love, of establishing ourselves upon God, of giving our lives for others as He gave His life for us. Holiness is to love from the glorious sacrifice of the cross, where total self-denial is found so that love, which gives everything on behalf of others, can express itself. The more that we stir ourselves into that glorious essence between our spirit and His Spirit, the more I cease being "me" in order to change into "us," and loving Him through loving others, the more I am drawn near to His holiness.

Sins against love, in any of its forms, touch the most delicate and sensitive area of the heart of the Father. Love is not an option. Outside of love there is only thick darkness, and it's terribly painful how we wound God. This is the commandment that Jesus gave us to keep:

A new commandment I give to you, that you love one another; as I have loved you, that you also love one another.
By this all will know that you are My disciples, if you have love for one another. John 13:34-35

Can a lost world, so needy of love, a world that cries in its loneliness and its deepest emptiness, see us as Christ's disciples when there is so much selfishness, so much division, so much judging and criticizing one other? Will we have the courage to see truth and cry out to understand the highest concept of the universe, which is the *Love of God,* greater and deeper than anyone can imagine?

Revelation is found in the Light, and Light flows out from His Love. The more the love, the more the revelation.

I have written in some of my books about the many different aspects of my experience within the heart of God[3] as the topic demanded it. But what I saw and understood behind that heavenly door requires many more books, and this is one of them.

God allowed me to see His throne, His Court of Righteousness and the myriads of angels who work together along with the Lord and the Church. In Heaven both dimensions are united. When we worship or intercede we become visible in the heavenly realm. Millions of tongues and nations emerge before the throne and are bathed in His Grace and Favor. Jesus Himself is the heavenly city from where the river of living water flows to nourish us and to give us life.

I stood in the very stage of the **Book of Revelation,** the most powerful revelation of Jesus as the King of kings and also the manual He gave us to rule and reign with Him. It's in this revelation of the prophetic dimensions where we can know Him with an unveiled face, where we are introduced to understand the mysteries of His Kingdom.

---

[3] *Seated in Heavenly Places* and *Eat of my flesh and Drink of my Blood.* By Ana Méndez Ferrell, published by AMF inc.

2 THE DILEMMA OF INTERPRETATION

1. THE TIMES WE LIVE IN

What times am I living in? What is God expecting of me and of this generation I am part of? What am I doing in this world…are all basic questions whose answer is based on what we believe about the end times.

What we believe about this fashions us and constrain us to make vital decisions. If everything will end in the upcoming years, then logically I will plan my life on a short-term basis. On the other hand, if this isn't so, then I will plan on leaving an inheritance for my children and my grandchildren.

If I believe Jesus will reign with His saints only after His *Second Coming*, then I would not aspire to have the blessings of His Kingdom until then. But if I believe that His Kingdom is already in the midst of us and that He is already ruling with His saints, then NOW is when I will do whatever it takes to partake in His blessings

Gaining full clarity and truth regarding this matter determines my purpose and my lifestyle. Therefore, this becomes imperatively important. This fixes our aim on whether we can receive from God today, or if we should only live in expectation of the future without really receiving anything while we are in this life.

I reached the conclusion that if my life and my destiny depend on my understanding of eschatology, then seeking the truth in the Bible and going deeper with God until He gives me the answers I am looking for is very important to me and is also my responsibility. This is also my exhortation for all of those that are seeking His truth.

Nowadays we find ourselves amidst a wave of terror that is being unleashed regarding the approaching "end of the world." We hear everywhere that the Earth will be destroyed; some talk about the rapture of the Church, while others think it is a mistaken interpretation of Scripture. At the end, the world sinks under doubts and fears, and the Church struggles to understand truth; some based on traditional teachings while others over what God is showing to the prophets of today. After my experience in *Patmos*, much of what I thought because of what I had been taught changed completely. To see the truths of the **Book of Revelation** from the heavenly perspective changed my life and my way of reading this Book.

I clearly understand that every revelation has to be confirmed by the Bible, therefore, I have spent years praying about these impressive truths I saw and experienced in the Kingdom of God dimensions, as to whether they were certain in the Word.

As a prophetess of God I have sought the answers to these

questions during almost 12 years of studying and receiving revelation. I sense a deep responsibility over this generation that God has called me to touch, and I desire to give them what I believe God has given me for them. *The Book of Revelation* is undoubtedly the most important one regarding this subject and the one I consider to be the most misinterpreted in our day.

God wants to open our understanding so we grasp His designs, His ways, and His thoughts.

This is why I am asking you to read this book with a humble and open spirit so you can understand things that will surely shake much of your theology regarding eschatology.[4]

I also encourage you to pray, seek, and ask the Lord to reveal to you as His child His divine truth; to question yourself as to why you believe what you believe about these subjects; and, if necessary, to make certain adjustments.

Then said he unto me, Fear not, Daniel: for from the first day that thou didst set thine heart to understand, and to chasten thyself before thy God, thy words were heard, and I am come for thy words.   Daniel 10:12

God loves to reveal Himself to a humble, willing heart and to take him or her to the depths of His knowledge and His revelation.

The Lord does not want to leave us at the level we are in He

---

[4] The word Eschatology means *"the study of the final events in Scripture. This science not only determines the things that will happen, but also our view of the present-day world. It will mold us and give substance to our thoughts."*

wants to take us to the measure of the stature of the perfect man which is Christ Jesus; He wants us to enter the fullness of the glory He has reserved for us. Many things that can be shaken must be shaken for this to happen, and, in this way, that which is immortal becomes manifest.

> *Whose voice then shook the earth: but now he hath promised, saying, Yet once more I shake not the earth only, but also heaven. And this word, Yet once more, signifieth the removing of those things that are shaken, as of things that are made, that those things which cannot be shaken may remain.* Hebrews 12:26, 27

2. INTERPRETATION OF THE *BOOK OF REVELATION*

Many books written on this subject are based on the interpretation of symbols and based on the preconceived idea of the destruction of the Earth. This is because the meaning of the word *apocalypse* is totally distorted in the dictionaries of many languages, English and Spanish among them.

Words carry concepts and ideologies that lead us to think in a certain manner and connect us to certain areas of the brain.

For example, if I hear the word *beauty* I will necessarily think about something pleasant and I will tune into that part of my brain where I perceive joy and happiness. If on the contrary I hear the word *abortion,* I will think about death, destruction, something that never succeeded and this will activate the pain center in the brain. The word *Apocalypse* **apokalupsis** is the Greek word, that means "revelation, apparition, coming, illumination, manifestation, bring to the light." Dictionaries however, translate it as: "the revelation of the end of the world, terrifying, horrible."[5]

In English it is interpreted as: "monumental catastrophe, total destruction, extinction, annihilation, death."[6]

Whether we like it or not, these incorrect definitions have conditioned our minds to interpret the **Book of Revelation** as a book of destruction, death and as the end of all created things.

This has produced an *end-of-the-world* concept in every culture. In every millennium and at every turn of the century the nations expect the world's final moment. Whether God will destroy the Earth or not is almost impossible to discern given the manner in which the consciousness of the world has conceived the tremendous grand finale.

What if God loves the Earth and the work of His hands and does not want to destroy it? Who is going to believe Him and come against such a forceful flow of mainstream thinking?

If, on the contrary, the **Book of Revelation** was, as its name indicates, a book of revelation of light, and of divine manifestation? How are we able to read it in this manner if the rest of the world wants to view it as something terrible?

The prophetic ministry has only been recognized as such in the last 30 to 40 years, and this, by very few. If the **Book of Revelation**

---

[5] *Strong's Concordance 602., ap-ok-al'-oop-sis;* from 601; disclosure: — appearing, coming, lighten, manifestation, be revealed, revelation.

[6] Oxford American Writer's Thesaurus

was analyzed by wise men who didn't have in them the Spirit of Prophecy, this necessarily must have caused interpretation errors. In many cases scholars have been reproducing what was taught to them generation after generation without even questioning where these theologies came from.

I have understood that the only way to genuinely hear God regarding anything is finding a totally neutral position. Massive mainstream thinking can lead us to err.

In 1999, when I was in the island of *Patmos* I was led to comprehend many things about this book. The fruit of those days opened my understanding to many truths. One of them has taken more than 12 years to begin unfurling and continue growing inside of me, and this is the revelation of the book of the *Apocalypse,* or the *Book of Revelation,* which I write about here.

3. HOW THE BOOK OF REVELATION WAS WRITTEN

The first thing I realized at the island, and based on serious research, was that John wrote this book during various sittings. He frequently went to the cave on the top of the hill, bringing with him one of his disciples named Prochorus[7] who would write the visions as John narrated them from the heavenly dimension.

---

[7] Historical fact documented in the Island of Patmos.

Apostle John receiving the revelation of Apocalypse while is written by his disciple Prochorus

As one enters this realm, one doesn't lose consciousness, so it is possible to talk about what we are seeing without coming back from the experience. The spirits of the prophets are subject to the prophets (1 Corinthians 14:32)!

THE ORDER OF THE CANON

When John's writings were discovered, they were not in order, and when the Canon of the New Testament was put together, these writings were accommodated as best they saw fit. This is why we find passages that apparently are in conflict with one another if we try to study this book from a chronological point of view. Some talk about a total destruction of the universe when the sixth seal is opened, but then at the end of Chapter 22 there's a call to come to salvation. Chapter 20 talks about a Final Judgment, but on the 22nd chapter we read about people who come to Christ for salvation. We also read about those who try to enter the city but cannot.

It is logical to suppose that after *THE* Final Judgment there will be no more room for the preaching of the Gospel or a place for those that are trying to force their way into the city.

We see yet another contradiction within the traditional chronological interpretation when *Babylon* falls in Chapter 11, then it falls again in Chapter 17, but its sentence is handed down in the 18th chapter. We see then the *Great Day of Wrath* falling upon the Earth and the sky rolling up as a scroll in Chapter 6, and yet in the 14th chapter the angel goes out to preach the Gospel.

If we put Chapters 21 and 22 after the Judgment we will never understand what Jesus already did for us in His First Coming and this is an absolute tragedy.

On the other hand, when the Bible Canon was put together in the fourth century, it was decided to put this **Book of Revelation** at the end. Like it or not, this order psychologically compels us to view it as the Book of "The End." If they had placed it after the Gospels, then maybe we would view it as truly the Kingdom Book Jesus left us. And if they had placed the Book of the Acts of the Apostles at the end, maybe the Church would still be full of life doing greater works than Jesus did, as He declared.

3   THE ESSENCE OF THE *BOOK OF REVELATION*

1. THE BOOK'S MAIN SUBJECT: THE REVELATION OF CHRIST

H eaven is timeless. God is the great I AM, the *Continuous Present.* In Heaven we can travel to the past in an instant and in the next be transferred to thousands of years into the future. Although there is no time in Heaven, it is not static either; it is impressively alive and active.

The book was written using a heavenly language and symbols that are not from Earth. It's the Kingdom of God's manual and legacy so we can govern with Jesus. The central theme in the *Book of Revelation* is "The Revelation of Jesus Christ." This is the name of the book and also its content.

> **The Revelation of Jesus Christ,** which God gave unto Him to show unto His servants things which must shortly come to pass. And He sent and signified it by His angel unto His servant John...   *Revelation 1:1*

It's not a book about the end of the world; it's a book on **how**

to know Jesus in His glory and about His government. It's a book that is alive in the Eternal Present **of God.** It's a book on government and about heavenly understanding. The Old Testament teaches us how God the Father reigned over the Earth while it was in a fallen state. The Father announces the things that will happen through the coming of His Son. The Ancient Covenant teaches us the character of the Father and His dealings with men through His people Israel.

The **Book of Revelation** is the government of the new Heaven and the new Earth, which have been redeemed by Messiah; it's the reign of Christ after He united Heaven and Earth in Him.

He hath made known unto us the mystery of His will, according to His good pleasure which He hath purposed in Himself, that in the dispensation of the fullness of times He might **gather together in one all things in Christ, both which are in heaven and which are on earth, even in Him.** *Ephesians 1:9-10*

It's the only book where God promises a blessing upon reading it because it is a book that teaches us how to live in the revelation of Christ in His eternity; it's the victory of His Kingdom imparting the most important tools for the saints to rule and judge together with Him.

It's not an obsolete book as some people assume, nor is it an unfulfilled book as others think. It contains something powerful regarding the revealed glory of Christ reserved for those who read it.

Blessed is he that readeth, and they that hear the words
of this prophecy, and keep those things which are written
therein; for the time is at hand.   *Revelation 1:3*

What blessedness could there be in reading this prophecy if it doesn't bring any life application for us now or for every believer throughout the ages?

2. JESUS MUST BE REVEALED TO EVERY BELIEVER

This is the revelation God gave John, but God reveals Himself to each one of us in a unique and singular manner according to our call and our position in the Kingdom.

The Church needs to be grounded in the revelation of Jesus Christ as Jesus told His disciples when He would ask them who did they say He was.

And Jesus answered and said unto him, 'Blessed art thou,
Simon Bar-Jonah, for flesh and blood hath not revealed
it unto thee, but My Father who is in Heaven. And I say
also unto thee, that thou art Peter, and upon this rock I
will build My church; and the gates of hell shall not prevail
against it.'   *Matthew 16:17-18*

The revelation of Christ directly given by the Holy Spirit is what lays the foundation for a Church that cannot be shaken by the gates of hell; this is what the **Book of Revelation** is all about.

Jesus Christ reveals Himself to John to give us the keys of His Kingdom and trains us to rule and to destroy the gates of hell.

3. THE PURPOSES OF THE BOOK

a) This is the Book of the Testimony of Jesus and the Realm of the Spirit

This is the most marvelous manual in the prophetic dimension, which is the testimony of Jesus. It's the revelation of the original blueprint from where all things were created. All the temple designs and its ordinances in the Ancient Covenant were only a type and shadow of the true ones in Heaven. This is the Book about the identity of Jesus as the sovereign King of the universe.

b) Victory Against Our Enemies

The essence of this book is the glory of Christ revealed to topple the structures of *Babylon*, which are the foundation of the devil's government.

This is a book that teaches us to defeat the enemy, to judge and to legislate in the dimensions of the Spirit, to change the destiny of our nations so these turn to God.

It teaches us how God judges from His throne and the diverse manners He does it, not as something that is accomplished on one single occasion but the manner and the instruments He uses to judge.

To reign means, among other things, to establish righteousness. This is what a righteous king does and we have been called to take the Kingdom of God and His righteousness throughout the Earth.

c) It Reveals Who We Are In Christ

It tells us who we are in Christ as priests and kings; what it means to be the **Tabernacle of God on Earth,** the *Jerusalem* from above, the *New Jerusalem* manifested in the temple not made with human hands but an Eternal One in the heavens and alive among the believers. In it, we understand the wonder of being married to Him not in the future but NOW.

d) It Shows Us The True Structure Of The Church

It's a book that talks to us about the design of God regarding His Church, its form, its structure, which is a cube and not a pyramid, along with its great power.

It teaches us to recognize how the structures of this world have been designed and how to destroy them to obtain the victory.

e) It Produces a Grandiose Fruit

It's a book that will mightily change your life, your destiny and the manner in which you perceive your Christianity.

To interpret it will require you to understand certain basic principles regarding the thinking and the heart of God. I will begin expounding on these foundational issues so light is shed for us to see the mysteries hidden in this marvelous book. To attempt to discern it based on words, symbols, analogies, or chronologies will only lead us to error since it is a heavenly book written from the Spirit of God in a spiritual language to the Spirit of His Church.

4. THE APOCALYPSE: THE KINGDOM MANUAL

a) Kings and Priests

The **Book of Revelation** is our Kingdom manual to govern jointly with Jesus. As we previously said, it is not a prophecy about the end of the world but the revelation of Jesus Christ in His glory. It is a heavenly book designed to let us know about the dimensions of Heaven and its operation on Earth. **The Church was born prophetic to be the voice of God and to reveal Him to the world.**

Jesus already ascended to the throne and sent His angel to John to instruct him about His government and how He would rule together with His saints and to let him know about the Church's glorious power.

From the beginning of the **Book of Revelation**, Jesus introduces Himself as Sovereign over the kings of the Earth and announces to us our heavenly rank as kings and priests. It's a message to be understood with a kingdom mentality.

*...and from Jesus Christ, who is the faithful witness, and the first-begotten of the dead, and the **(sovereign) prince over the kings of the earth.** Unto Him that loved us, and washed us from our sins in His own blood, and hath made us **kings and priests** unto God and His Father, to Him be glory and dominion forever and ever. Amen.*

Revelation 1:5-6

He wants to train us to reign and to be priests unto His Father.

The first lesson is that Jesus, before being crowned King, had to be a Priest. This is the Mediator between God and man, the One who ministers and makes the Heavenly Father tangible and visible. He brings the truths and the essence of Heaven and manifests them in our midst. A priest is one who sacrifices unto the Lord. Jesus was the ultimate sacrificer through His death at the cross. He is the faithful witness because He reproduces in a reliable manner everything the Father does and speaks.

Jesus is the High Priest of the good things of the coming age, which are the new Earth and the new Heavens.

But Christ, having come a High Priest of good things to come, by a greater and more perfect tabernacle, not made with hands (that is to say, not of this building)...
Hebrews 9:11

He did not minister the earthly things as the priests of the Old Covenant did, but the heavenly ones that were about to come to Earth.

He was then exalted in glory to reign in the tabernacle not made by human hands but the Eternal one in the heavens.

In like manner we have to understand **our mission of manifesting the Father** so the world can be reconciled to Him. This will depend on whether or not Christ is revealed in our hearts, and this is what gives us authority to have the same dominion Adam had.

It's the Revelation of Christ that gives us access to the keys of the Kingdom and lays the foundation so the gates of hades do not prevail against us. (Mathew 16:17-19)

The *Book of Revelation* is the revelation God gave to John, but God has one for each of us who will manifest the message with the tools we need to exercise our service as kings.

For this to happen we need to learn to "be in the Spirit" just like John, since our kingdom is from the spiritual spheres.

I was in the Spirit on the Lord's Day, and I heard behind me a great voice as of a trumpet...   Revelation 1:10

John was trained to hear the voice of God and knew that if he was able to hear Him, then he could also see Him. He heard Him from his spirit with great expectation, knowing that Jesus continually manifested Himself unto him.

He was 'in the Spirit' on the Lord's Day. When we enter into Him, we are introduced to the great "I Am" in the *Continuous Present* of the presence of God. In there, time ceases to exist, past and future.

We enter into the Eternal of His Being on the Lord's day, a place where there is no time. Therefore, when John says 'I was on the *Lord's Day'*, he wanted to say he was on God's time, inside the realm where He IS and where He manifests Himself. The Spirit of Prophecy is the testimony of Jesus.

The *Book of Revelation* is the **Testimony of Jesus.** For this reason it cannot be interpreted from the mindset of Earth but can only be interpreted from being inside Him. 'I was In the Spirit,' that's how this book was written, entering the spiritual dimension of Heaven, into God's realm.

Likewise when we learn to be **IN** His Spirit, His power is revealed to us to be born and live in the sphere of His dominion.

b) It's the individual revelation of Christ in His glory that gives authority to the Church.

When the Father revealed the identity of the Christ to Simon Peter, it led him to possess the keys of the Kingdom. Jesus talks about the same to John in the *Book of Revelation.* He displays Himself to him as holding the keys of *death and hades.* Therefore, the vivid revelation of Christ in your life will give you the keys to govern.

Upon his return from *Patmos,* John confronted the powers of Diana of the Ephesians, and the temple of the goddess crumbled down. While at the island, he also defied the power of Kynops as we mentioned before.

The revelation of Jesus in His glory makes John fall as dead (Revelation 1:17). It takes a lot of hard work for many people to die to their flesh and to the world because Jesus has never been revealed to them in this manner.

The truth is that when this happens to you, the radiance and love that emanate from Him is such that you want nothing else of this world; you remain marked forever.

You have to see Him in all His glory, living and reigning inside of you, fusing with your spirit and becoming ONE with you. Only by dying to your flesh will you be able to see Him in the right proportion of Who He is in your life. Everything

He is needs to captivate every part of your being. You have to see Him in all His majesty until you fall to the ground as Peter did during the miraculous fishing incident, and tell Him, *stay away from me for I am a sinner.* It's in this position that Jesus can teach you to be a king without the danger of your becoming proud.

It's in this position from where He reveals the whole dimension of His Kingdom. Heaven cannot be interpreted; it has to reveal itself to us. **Therein lies the difference, to know the truths in the Book of Revelation.** The *Book of Revelation* is based on Old Testament prophecy revealed from Heaven by the same Spirit of prophecy, which is Jesus, who is the steadfast anchor of our understanding.

4 THE POWER OF PRECONCEIVED IDEAS

At the time Jesus came to Earth, the scribes, the doctors of the Law and priests were all learned men in the Law, yet failed to recognize the coming of Messiah. The reason was that they had studied the Scriptures so much that they had set their preconceived ideas over and above God's revelation, and even though they had the Son of God in front of them, they failed to see Him as such.

Their idea of Messiah coming in a chariot of fire from Heaven just as Elijah had left was so deeply rooted in their minds that when He was born in a stable (a Succoth tent) in *Bethlehem*, the son of a carpenter, it became impossible for them to believe it. This simply did not fit with their theologies. A child conceived by a virgin out of wedlock? What manner of insanity was this! They were expecting a King coming in a chariot who would defeat the Romans and would sit on the throne of David here in the earthly *Jerusalem*.

But this Jesus had not come to sit on a throne of this world. His kingdom was not of this world. They were confused; they wanted a kingdom here at all costs not at an unknown dimension.

*Therefore Pilate entered again into the Praetorium, and summoned Jesus and said to Him, 'Are You the King of the Jews?' Jesus answered, 'My kingdom is not of this world. If My kingdom were of this world, then My servants would be fighting so that I would not be handed over to the Jews; but as it is, **My kingdom is not of this realm.'** Therefore Pilate said to Him, "So You are a king?" Jesus answered, "You say correctly that I am a king. For this I have been born, and for this I have come into the world, to testify to the truth. Everyone who is of the truth hears My voice."* John 18:33, 36, 37

*Now when He was asked by the Pharisees when the kingdom of God would come, He answered them and said, "The kingdom of God does not come with observation; nor will they say, 'See here!' or 'See there!'. **For indeed, the kingdom of God is within you."*** Luke 17:20-21

They couldn't stand this truth! According to them, the Messiah that was to come was a king that would save them and reign on David's physical throne. They couldn't conceive of an invisible kingdom so therefore they crucified him.

This compels me to think carefully: why did the theologians in Israel, who back then were great scholars, meticulous in the use of jots and tittles, miss it?

A 4000 – year - old scriptural legacy tradition failed them for the discerning of the prophecy. Why? Because they had it all figured out ahead of time and when God did things according to His way

48

and not theirs, they couldn't change their way of thinking.

God had to resort to gentile magicians from the East, shepherds who were keeping the night watch, and Joseph and Mary's few close friends and relatives. These were not great theologians, scribes, or doctors, but simple people who would believe when they saw the heavens open and the angels talking to them (Luke 2:8-14).

God always seeks the simple-hearted, those who are capable of changing their paradigms when He reveals Himself; those who acknowledge before Him that they do not know all things. And if God is taking us from light to light and from glory to glory, necessarily there will be things that will be revealed to us in a different manner from what we used to believe and we need to have the spiritual ability to make the adjustments.

Blessed are the pure in heart, For they shall see God.
Matthew 5:8

a) Jesus Opens Our Understanding

The scribes and the doctors of the Law were not the only ones who failed to understand the Scriptures; it got to a point that even Jesus' disciples ran into the wall and had no understanding either.

After living with Him during three years and seeing all His wonders, Jesus had to open their understanding so they could understand the Scriptures. The time they spent with Him and were discipled and trained did not enable them to understand the Scriptures.

49

After His resurrection, Jesus appeared to two of his disciples on the road to *Emaus* and they did not recognized Him in His incorruptible body until He parted the bread and their eyes were opened. From there they headed to where the others had gathered, to tell them the great news.

And He said unto them, 'These are the words which I spoke unto you while I was yet with you, that all things must be fulfilled which were written in the Law of Moses and in the Prophets and in the Psalms concerning Me.' Then opened He their understanding, **that they might understand the Scriptures...** *Luke 24:44-45*

We see two impressive things here. The first one is His opening of their understanding to understand Scripture, and the second is His revelation of how **everything that was written about Him in the Torah, in Psalms and the prophets had been fulfilled.**

In English it's hard to grasp because the auxiliary verb "must" is the same in present, future and in past tense, yet in the original Greek and in other languages it says, "… had been fulfilled."

These two truths are relevant to the subjects we are touching on. Unless Jesus opens our understanding to understand Scripture, we will find ourselves in the same condition as the scribes, doctors of the Law and Jesus' disciples.

Jesus holds in Himself the perfect interpretation of Scripture, and He tells us that everything pertaining to Him has already been fulfilled. Using passages from Isaiah, Daniel, and Zechariah saying there are certain things not yet fulfilled is a doctrinal error.

Just as Jesus' disciples hit a wall that wouldn't allow them to understand Scripture, we may likewise find ourselves in this same situation.

I feel that there is nothing more dangerous than to cling to a prophetic interpretation and say, "This is how it is and I am not budging."

What makes us think that we are incapable of being wrong when the great ccribes and doctors of the Law failed so miserably?

They were sincerely mistaken, yet their theologies and preconceived ideas were more important to them than God Himself.

I ask you to pray at this moment for Jesus Christ Himself to open your understanding to perceive the scripture in the *Book of Revelation* as He alone can reveal it unto you.

Ask Him for eyes to see what you couldn't see before, and ears to hear His Spirit clearly.

Through this book we will find out what the reality of the Kingdom is and we will analyze many Scriptural passages that will fill us with light to understand what Jesus did in His *First Coming.*

The Holy Spirit will change our manner of thinking so we may be used as the kings and priests we represent for God the Father, seeing the inheritance of light and revelation in the **Apocalypse, the Book of Revelation.** Then, we will fill the Earth with the knowledge of the glory of God as the waters cover the sea.

THE TWO GREAT ERAS

1.- PATMOS, SECOND VISION

I found myself inside the Holy of Holies of God's heart, the place from where life and the greatest love of the entire universe flows. The Holiness of Love shone with such brilliance, it pierced me and sanctified me at the same time. Everything that is within me became holy in that place because no uncleanliness can remain there.

I was moved by a combination of pain and joy. On one end I saw his wounds caused by each one of us and on the other end, the love that would exude from that place, which far from blaming me, attracted me to Him to sanctify me and to love me. My spirit, which I was able to see in that place, was filled with a light that enabled me to know many things at the same time. I could see towards different directions and I could see many doors, but not like those on Earth, they were placed on different planes, and each one led to a different dimension.

Around God's heart were the doors that came from the sufferings of Christ; every shed drop of blood, each sore borne into his flesh formed a door. It's impossible to enter into each one of these during a human being's lifetime, but those we are granted to enter lead to marvelous places of His wisdom, His intelligence, His power, His riches, and His glory.

Heaven is multidimensional; it's not like Earth where all we see with our natural eyes is the visible realm. There is no up or down, no before or after, everything simply "is" in each one of the infinite dimensions and manifestations of God.

In Heaven everything is agile, light, weightless, and spacious. There is no way to describe the beauty seen in the dimensions of light. The Holy Spirit attracted my attention to one of the doors on one of those flesh-like walls that composed the most sensitive parts of His heart. More than a door, it was like a large gash whose edges were ripped open. I approached it and a severely intense pain filled me to my innards. "Enter" said the Lord. I had barely set foot when I was transported to a very different place, atop a high mountain from where the Garden of Eden could be seen. It was the moment right before the fall.

Everything was full of the love of God and He rejoiced in loving His family, the children He had created. He made them out of the same love substance that flows from His Holy of Holies. They were just like Him in the terrestrial domain. Suddenly, everything began to vibrate in strange manner and a black shadow entered Eden and took the form of a serpent. The dialogue of death ensued, which produced the fall, and then silence fell. A deep hollow akin to a black hole in space formed around Adam and his wife. Then came a frightful thundering from Heaven and an intense outcry of pain paralyzed the universe. I turned to see where that terrible sound came from, and instantly I saw how the Father's heart was being rent. He had lost his beloved children, His dearest family, in an instant. It's difficult to describe such a pain. Only when we have loved with all our hearts and lose the one we love can we feel a fragment of what the Father felt. There was silence for a long time. Everything was arrested in an uncontrollable pain. No angel dared to move.

The whole Earth became covered by deep darkness, and the pain of death and separation enshrouded the Earth's surface while a deep chasm isolated it from the heavens. Man ended up condemned to a life in the shadows of death and darkness. Sheol had opened its mouth, and sickness, distress, poverty, hate, hopelessness, sadness and evil filled the world. The terror of death had taken over the hearts of humanity.

Seen from Heaven, the Earth resembled a parched land covered by thorns. Deep darkness seeped from hell and enabled it to prevail, producing an unquenchable thirst in all men. The denseness of the deep darkness covering the Earth could be seen and felt. The frequency of the land was heavy; the sound was grave and strident, chaotic like the roar of frightened wild animals. That density can never penetrate the acute lightness of Heaven's frequency.

I cried as I felt the pain of death in God's heart throughout my body. But something happened that moved me to happiness. From that same torn heart I saw a light come forth. It was the light of Jesus, the love that never ceases to be; the Spirit of Prophecy that was coming from Heaven announcing the marvelous plan of Salvation. The light began taking form before my eyes. It became a great mountain from where milk and honey would flow, and from here, also new wine flowed, having such a fragrance that it filled the whole place. A beautiful fountain of clear waters, shimmering with lights as stars navigating amidst it, opened up; there were also tongues of fire dancing over them. I saw how rivers formed and streamed downwards and became a great river that flooded an enormous valley. I knew then that mountain was Jesus Himself.

I then saw other mountains being fashioned from the great mountain; waters of life, honey, and new wine flowed from each one and filled the Heaven as far as my eye could see.[9] All of these that joined to the great mountain were also Jesus, but as I saw this, He still had not descended to Earth, which remained parched and in pain.

I remained there gazing for a long time. I don't know how long, since there is no time in Heaven, and a moment in my consciousness can equal millenniums up there. At that moment, an elderly man appeared next to me; his face was beaming and his garments were wine red. I knew he was one of the 24 elders that are before the throne. He gave me a key and told me, "this is the key of knowledge." When I held it in my hands I felt a very strong unction that encased me, and my eyes were filled with light. I could see various dimensions at the same time without moving anywhere.

I then saw how other types of heavens were formed between the Earth and God's Heaven. These heavens were of deep darkness and a great city began forming within it, resembling a gigantic

---

[9] Scriptures that confirm this vision: Joel 3:18 y Zechariah 13:1

beast full of internal structures. It had tentacles that appeared as pipeline-encased roadways that led to thousands of cities of darkness that received nourishment from the mother city.

There were also diverse dimensions and doors in those heavens that led some to Earth, and others to the depths of hell. Seven mountains also surrounded the city, all of them sinister-looking, craggy and parched. They were filled with caves that led to thousands of prisons. Both the cities and the mountains were teeming with demons, and there were thrones over the summits of these mountains. These were covered by structures resembling transparent vaults that protected them so no one could tear them down.

I was still looking at all of this when there came a great music from Heaven, like myriads of angels together with the majestic sound from the wings of the cherubim that resounded in all the celestial universe. Following the music, thunder and lightning were heard and the whole sky was clouded with the presence of the Most High. A resplendent light began to whirl inside the cloud becoming more and more magnificent until it took a form and turned into a human fetus. He began to grow inside a woman, it was Mary's womb. In the Spirit He appeard as full of light surrounded by water and blood, and a rainbow enveloped him. He was born and became a child, then a man.

I was seeing in the the heavens the moment Jesus became flesh and then lived among us. Time is no more in that place, and everything appears to occur in instants. Blood enveloped him completely and He began to be condensed as a liquid cloud until He transformed into the perfect cornerstone rock that gleamed as a clear and extremely luminous diamond, which remained floating in the middle of the universe. It was like seeing the crucifixion from another dimension. the place where the power of His blood transformed into His very own glory.

From this rock came an explosion, and its shock waves covered the heavens with light as when a star forms. I then saw one resembling the Son of Man in the midst of the diamond and seated in a throne full of splendor. His Glory covered the Earth and it was filled with His Praise; from the throne a voice came saying, "It is done." Jesus was now seated at the right hand of His Father, on His throne.

This was the heavenly vision God gave me of what happened in one of the heavenly dimensions when Jesus came to Earth, and then ascended back to His Father. This fact changed everything in the Universe. The Earth once again was filled with the presence of God. Heaven and Earth once again were united in Jesus.

He who descended is also the One who ascended far above all the heavens, that He might fill all things.
Ephesians 4:10

The first heavens passed away; these were the heavens where the throne of redemption had not yet been occupied. The former Earth also passed away, the Earth of deep darkness, death, and pain, everything was filled with Jesus, with His light. I then saw a new Earth and a new Heaven. It was the same Earth, the beautiful planet God made and loved, but now it was filled with His glory, with His presence. A crystalline coating of the blood of Jesus was wrapped around it, and the Holy Spirit filled it with

His luminosity and Wisdom, making the Father accessible to all who seek Him. The holy mountain with its springs of waters was established over the Earth to all who want to drink from it. Its rainbow shines forever, uniting Heaven and Earth, which shall never again be destroyed. The Earth is no longer the old Earth covered by darkness, dryness and without hope, it's a new Earth and a new Heaven because the righteousness bought for us at the price of the cross now dwells in it. Jesus, the promised Messiah, became flesh and came to Earth, and changed the heavens and the Earth forever, and His Kingdom shall never end.

Everything has been done, but some things need to be manifested from the invisible to the visible.

As His righteousness and justice become established through a generation of true sons of God, we will see a better Earth, with the glory that we all expect to see. The divine design of His magnificent city will also be seen in every city that converts to Jesus, the King of kings.

He will soon bring judgments that will destroy the wicked and will reward the true righteous. People will come to know God, and the Earth will be filled with the knowledge of the glory of God as the waters cover the sea.

2. THE KEY OF UNDERSTANDING

This vision, along with receiving the key of understanding that is given to all who want to know Jesus and seek to walk in His Kingdom, changed my way of reading Scripture. As I mentioned in theprevious chapter, Jesus told His disciples that everything that had been written about Him in the Law of Moses, the Psalms, and the Prophets has already been fulfilled. Jesus is THE SPIRIT OF PROPHECY (Revelation 19:10), and He is the One who spoke through all his prophets.

> *Of which salvation the prophets have enquired and searched diligently, who prophesied of the grace that should come unto you: Searching what, or what manner of time the Spirit of Christ which was in them did signify, when it testified beforehand the sufferings of Christ, and the glory that.*   *1 Peter 1:10-11*

If He said everything had been fulfilled, then this is the anchor of revelation and interpretation. The Bible is divided into two great sections, which clearly mark out two eras and two distinct covenants of God's dealings with men. Since the fall of Adam, the Scriptures announce the coming of Messiah as the solution to the deep darkness that had settled in to reign over the Earth.

The Father had **one single Redeeming Plan** with His Son, the Messiah through whom He would restore all things to their original state in the *Garden of Eden*. God created man to rule and have dominion on Earth through fellowship with his Creator and this is what Jesus came to restore. His redeeming work concluded at the cross of Calvary. He clearly stated, "It is finished." The Kingdom of God was established when Jesus ascended to Heaven and sat at the right hand of the Father to reign together with His Body, which is the Church.

> *To him that overcometh, will I grant to sit with Me on My throne, even as I also overcame and **am set down with My Father on His throne**.*   *Revelation 3:21*

This plan of redemption is announced throughout the entire history of the Old Testament. This was to bring a new phase, a new century, a new era full of God where His designs were to be established.

Messiah would bring about the glory that Adam once lost, it would be manifested again in the sons and daughters of God.

*Arise, shine, for thy light is come, and the glory of the LORD is risen upon thee. For behold, **the darkness shall cover the earth and gross darkness the people;** but the LORD shall arise upon thee, and His glory shall be seen upon thee. And the Gentiles shall come to thy light, and kings to the brightness of thy rising.*

Isaiah 60:1-3

This is news of great joy! God was to change the government over all the Earth. The coming of Messiah would neither be a partial victory nor one of phases. It was to be radical! Culminating! Extremely powerful! It would crush the head of the devil forever! It would snatch the keys of death and hell, and it would seat Him as King of kings over the whole Earth forever.

Jesus came to change the era of deep darkness into an era of light. He came to substitute that which was only a type and shadow for what is true. He came to bring a New Covenant, a new government that would change the heavens and the Earth completely. The Spirit of Christ prophesied two great eras, which even the unbelievers acknowledge: *Before Christ* and *After Christ.*

Allow me to elaborate further on this concept. We are looking at a clear division between two great eras:

- One of darkness and one of redemption
- An Old Covenant and a New Covenant.
- The earthly things that were a shadow of what was to come, and the heavenly ones that are His Kingdom on Earth.
- The Heavens separated from man and the heavens united with man.
- The old creature and the new creature.
- Old things passed away and all things made new.
- The earthly *Jerusalem* in the Old Covenant, the *Jerusalem* above in the New Covenant.
- The old wine skins and the new wineskins. (God's people in the Old Testament and God's people in the New)
- The old wine and the new wine.
- The former Levitical Priesthood and the new Priesthood according to the Order of Melchizedek.

If we do not understand the first and grandiose *First Coming* of Messiah and the power it brings, that He is already seated on His throne, we will continue waiting for Him to come to do what He already did, which is a wrong perception of the *second coming.*

I will go into detail about the work of Messiah in Chapter 7, where many issues that are still surrounded in much confusion shall become clear to us.

Before going into a full interpretation of the **Book of Revelation,** I feel it's important to itemize and understand previously mentioned principles in the heart of God, which are keyt o understanding it.

SECTION II

THE FUNDAMENTAL THEMES IN
THE BOOK OF REVELATION

T he central theme in the **Book of Revelation** is the *Revelation of Jesus Christ as Sovereign King of the Universe.* Shortly before the great judgment over *Jerusalem* in the year 70 A.D.and before the *Roman Empire* was destroyed, Jesus appeared to John in ALL His glory.

The new century was about to begin: the age of light and of the manifestation of Christ in the heart of the believers. Before His ascension, Jesus spent 40 days teaching the disciples about the Kingdom of God. He was about to go up to Heaven and take the throne of Majesty on High, and Hewanted to make it very clear for them to understand what was about to happen after his departure. His Kingdom was to be established in the midst of men when the Holy Spirit descended upon all flesh. God is One, and He would come to occupy Earth once again.

God left them basic principles on what He was about to do on Earth; if we understand them, they will steer us into revelation. The comprehension of biblical prophecy is not an issue of understanding or a play on words, but instead an understanding the global principle in God's thinking. On the other hand, we must also consider the *Time* when it was written and to *Whom* it was spoken. And even though the whole Scripture is alive and a spiritual tool for the Church, it was written and addressed primarily to the people of Israel.

Jesus left us with nine basic themes, or fundamental principles that we need to understand them to interpret the prophecy in the ***Book of Revelation:***

1. New Heaven and new Earth
2. The Work of Messiah in His *First Coming*
3. God's Tabernacle with men
4. The *New Jerusalem*
5. The Wedding Feast of the Lamb
6. The Destruction of *Babylon*
7. The Reigning of Christ
8. The Abode of God in the Clouds
9. The Supreme Court of God's Judgments

Following these primary themes, we encounter four secondary themes derived from the first ones that give us the details of how Heaven and Earth operate in harmony: 1) the heavenly battles, 2) the tribulations, 3) the organization of the kingdom of darkness against the light, and 4) the operation of the diverse angels.

6 A NEW HEAVEN AND A NEW EARTH

I n the previous chapter we established the division of the
two major periods or eras that shape Biblical history in the
Old Testament and the Messianic era. This understanding
serves as a guideline to interpret the *first basic theme* which is what
Scripture refers as the "new Heaven" and "new Earth".

> And I saw a new Heaven and a new Earth, for the first
> heaven and the new earth had passed away.
>
> *Revelation 21:1a*

1. DOES GOD WANT TO DESTROY THE EARTH?

God loves the Earth, which He filled with His glory through His
Son, and does not want to destroy it. He entered into covenant
with Noah, and that covenant remains forever.

> And I will remember My covenant which is between Me
> and you and every living creature of all flesh, and the
> waters shall no more become a flood to destroy all flesh.
> And the rainbow shall be in the cloud; and I will look upon
> it, that I may remember the everlasting covenant between

God and every living creature of all flesh that is upon the earth. *Genesis 9:15-16*

God would not enter into an eternal covenant with man and creation to not destroy them again by water but then to destroy everything by fire. That would be like ironically saying, "I enter into a covenant with you not to kill you by the sword but I will now kill you with a gun." God does not act in that fashion.

God will judge those who destroy the Earth because He loves it and does not want to see it destroyed.

*And the nations were angry; and Thy wrath is come, and the time of the dead, that they should be judged, and that Thou shouldest give reward unto Thy servants the prophets, and to the saints and them that fear Thy name, small and great, **and shouldest destroy them that destroy the earth.*** *Revelation 11:18*

One generation passeth away, and another generation cometh; but the earth abideth forever. *Ecclesiastes 1:4*

*And He built His sanctuary like high palaces, like the Earth which **He hath established forever.*** *Psalm 78:69*

*Thy people also shall be all righteous; **they shall inherit the land forever,** the branch of My planting, the work of My hands, that I may be glorified.* *Isaiah 60:21*

2. THE BURNING ELEMENTS

The conflict arises when people read Chapter 3 in Peter's second epistle where it seems to be talking about the Earth burning up in flames. This is but a bad translation in our languages. The Bible needs to be coherent in itself. Initially, this passage talks about the destruction of the wicked.

Fire in Scripture means "judgment." When Scripture talks about a *fire baptism* or that *we shall be tried by fire*, it doesn't mean we will literally burn away. Fire is a purifying instrument. God wants to cleanse the Earth and purify it by judging the ungodly people.

*But the Day of the Lord will come as a thief in the night, in which the **heavens** shall pass away with a great noise, and the **elements** shall melt with fervent heat. The earth also and the works that are therein shall be burned up. Seeing then that all these things shall be dissolved, what manner of persons ought ye to be in all holy manner of living and godliness, looking for and hastening unto the coming of the Day of God, wherein the **heavens,** being on fire, shall be dissolved and the **elements** shall melt with fervent heat? Nevertheless we, according to His promise, look for new heavens and a new earth, **wherein dwelleth righteousness.*** 2 Peter 3: 10-13

We have some key words in this portion that help us interpret it correctly. The first one is *heavens*. This is the Greek word **ouranos,**[10]

---

[10] ***Strong's concordance 3772, ouranos´;*** perhaps from the same as 3735 (through the idea of elevation); the sky; by extension, heaven (as the abode of God); by implication, happiness, power, eternity; specially, the Gospel (Christianity): — air, heaven(-ly), sky.

which means an *elevated place.* It refers to the high places, to the *second heaven,* the place from where the powers of darkness reign and induce man to ungodliness. It does not refers to the destruction of the universe. This is cleared up with the second word I highlighted: *elements.* In Greek it is **stoicheion,**[11] which means "structure, foundation, rudiment." This is where the word in English *stoic* is derived, which means "affirmed with utmost assurance".

Now this word does not refer to the physical elements of universal matter, but to the structures of this world that have ruled over the Earth and that Jesus came to topple. Apostle Peter concludes afterwards that upon destroying these world structures we will enjoy a new Heaven and a new Earth where righteousness dwells. We do not have to wait for the supposed "end of the world" for the righteousness of God to reign on Earth. His Kingdom is righteousness, peace, and joy in the Holy Ghost, and it's already in our midst.

This whole passage acquires greater clarity as we continue reading.

And account that the longsuffering of our Lord is salvation, even as our beloved brother **Paul also, according to the wisdom given unto him, hath written unto you, as also in all his epistles, speaking in them of these things. Therein are some things hard to understand,** *which those who are unlearned and unstable wrest, as they*

---

[11] ***Strong's Concordance 4747 . stoicheion;*** neuter of a presumed derivative of the base of 4748; something orderly in arrangement, i.e. (by implication) a serial (basal, fundamental, initial) constituent (literally), proposition (figuratively): — element, principle, rudiment.

do also the other Scriptures, unto their own destruction.
2 Peter 3:15-16

We see Peter here quoting Apostle Paul who talks about these things in almost all of his epistles. This is exceedingly key since NOWHERE in his epistles does Paul talk about the Earth burning up and being destroyed. However, he does talk about the removing of those things that can be shaken in almost all of them (*Book of Hebrews,* if Paul is in effect the author).

And these words, 'yet once more,' signifieth the removing of those things which can be shaken, such as things that are made, that those things which cannot be shaken may remain.   *Hebrews 12:27*

He writes about the structures of darkness that must be vanquished by the believer who must subject them through Jesus' Victory and put them under his/her feet.

He tells us about how these structures have already been sentenced and everything in Heaven and Earth has been made **new.**

Therefore if any man be in Christ, he is a new creature: old things are passed away; behold, all things have become new.   *2 Corinthians 5:17*

Peter exhorted the believers to live in a holy manner because all the structures of wickedness were to be judged in his time, and, along with them, those who partake of them. Further on I will talk about prophetic times and will analyze the part that talks about

71

how *a day is like a thousand years and a thousand years like a day.* For the time being I am focusing on the meaning of a *new Heaven* and a *new Earth.*

In Peter's passage we saw how righteousness dwells in this new Heaven and new Earth. Let's look at the analogous passages from the Old Testament, which enlighten us as to its interpretation. Peter was not talking about anything new; he was quoting the Scripture in Isaiah 65 where Jehovah had already prophesied these things.

3. ISAIAH'S PROPHECY

Let's remember how Jesus opened His disciples' understanding so they could understand how EVERYTHING that had been prophesied about Him had already been fulfilled.

For, behold, I create new heavens and a new earth; and **the former shall not be remembered, nor come into mind.** *But be ye glad and rejoice for ever in that which I create; for behold, I create Jerusalem a rejoicing, and her people a joy. And I will rejoice in Jerusalem, and joy in My people; and the voice of weeping shall be no more heard in her, nor the voice of crying. There shall be no more thence an infant of days, nor an old man that hath not filled his days; for the child shall die a hundred years old; but the sinner being a hundred years old shall be accursed. And they shall build houses and inhabit them; and they shall plant vineyards and eat the fruit of them. They shall not build and another inhabit; they shall not plant and another eat; for as the days of a tree are the days of My* *people, and Mine elect shall long enjoy the work of their hands. They shall not labor in vain, **nor bring forth for trouble;** for they are the seed of the blessed of the LORD, and their offspring with them. And it shall come to pass, that before they call, I will answer; and while they are yet speaking, I will hear. The wolf and the lamb shall feed together, and the lion shall eat straw like the bullock; and dust shall be the serpent's meat. They shall not hurt nor destroy in all My holy mountain," saith the LORD."*

Isaiah 65:17-25

When we read this passage with the preconceived idea that the Earth will be destroyed along with the entire universe, we imagine a new celestial planet. We are unable to conceive this to be true for today because the Church continues weeping, continues getting sick, many die young and millions are in lack. In the natural we are not seeing the wolf and the lamb feeding together or children that die a hundred years old. We therefore develop a theology according to *what we don't have* and not according to what was already paid for us at the cross.

The New Testament declares that old things have passed away and all things have been made new and this points again to the two eras: the old and the new.

"I bring joy to Jerusalem and rejoicing to her people" are promises that have to do with Messiah's *first coming*. He himself spoke it when He declared to them that the Spirit of the Lord was upon Him to bring the good news, liberty to the captives and joy to those in mourning. (Luke 4:18)

The key passage related to this is Isaiah 65:23: *They shall not labor in vain or **bring forth children for sudden terror or calamity;** for they shall be the descendants of the blessed of the Lord, and their offspring with them.*

If we part from the erroneous idea that this passage refers to a new celestial planet, we find ourselves in a conflict. How come it says here we will no longer bring forth children for calamity? Those who have interpreted this passage in this way also say that in this new Earth the children of God shall have a resurrected body, resembling that of the angels, who can no longer bear children.

*But they which shall be counted worthy to obtain that world and the resurrection from the dead, neither marry, nor are given in **marriage:***
Neither can they die any more: for they are equal unto the angels; and are the children of God, being the children of the resurrection.   *Luke 20:35-36*

This passage therefore has nothing to do with a new planet but with a new Heaven and a new Earth in Jesus; with the rulership of the King of kings Who now governs the Earth.

On one end, when Jesus makes us "new creatures," He doesn't have to physically destroy us, we are made new in our spirit and in our soul. The same thing therefore applies for the Earth to be made "new", it doesn't have to burn up and disappear from the universe; it's renewed by the glory of Jesus who fills it all in all.

74

a) There Will Be No More Weeping

Now, why does it say there will be no more weeping? This refers to the ensuing terrible pain when people died in the time before the coming of Messiah. Death had not been vanquished, and the idea of dying was dreadful. When a loved one died, it was devastating to think they had gone to a gloomy, cold, and abysmal place. The idea per se was unbearable to the hearts of men, but Jesus came and defeated death. Today, those of us who belong to Him, even though we undergo a necessary period of mourning for our soul to adjust to the loss, we rejoice that our loved ones are in Heaven with the Lord if they were saved. God is not a God of the dead but of the living and our beloved who departed in Christ are alive and not dead.

Jesus had the fullness of the Deity in Him. He was One with the Father. He was the Kingdom of God walking among the living and, regardless, He wept when Lazarus died and when He predicted the destruction of *Jerusalem*. In the Kingdom of God, in the new Earth and in the new Heaven He gave us, every tear is wiped away.

b) For The Child Shall Die A Hundred Years Old

Why, then, did Isaiah say, 'for the child shall die a hundred years old'? This speaks about longevity and the power of resurrection that indwells the true believer, who has been born of the Spirit.

And so it is written, "The first man Adam became a living being." The last Adam became a life-giving spirit.
1 Corinthians 15:45

In like manner, when death reigns in those who do not have Christ, it progresses until it deteriorates their bodies and takes them away; resurrection reigns over those who believe, quickening and rejuvenating their mortal body.

c) The Wolf And The Lamb

The wolf and the lamb shall feed together, and the lion shall eat straw like the bullock; and dust shall be the serpent's meat. They shall not hurt nor destroy in all My holy mountain, saith the LORD."   Isaiah 65:25

This is a type of the Church and the different personalities in people who draw near to the Kingdom of God. We call Jesus a lamb and also a lion. He said He would send us out as sheep among wolves. These wolves refers to those who were evil people, but then convert, then come into the Kingdom and dwell together with us.

Zephaniah talks to us about this same zoo morphology:

Her princes in her midst are roaring lions; Her judges are evening wolves, that leave not a bone till morning.
Zephaniah 3:3

If we open our hearts, we will be able to grasp for ourselves these truths God already bestowed upon us. But if we see them as a reality for a new planet, we shall never possess the fullness of what Jesus did for us.

... and hath raised us up together and made us sit together in heavenly places in Christ Jesus...   *Ephesians 2:6*

76

THE WORK OF MESSIAH IN HIS FIRST COMING

1. THE DEVIL STOLE FROM US THE GLORY AND THE ESSENCE OF THE FIRST COMING.

T his is our second basic *theme* of interpretation that is needed to understand the truths of the **Book of Revelation.**

And I heard a loud voice saying in Heaven, 'Now have come salvation and strength, and the Kingdom of our God, and the power of His Christ; for the accuser of our brethren is cast down, who accused them before our God day and night.' Revelation 12:10

Part of the problem we find ourselves in is that in many cases there is no clarity as to what the objective of Christ's First Coming was.

Most Christians are awaiting with great expectation the *Second Coming* of Christ, hoping it will be sooner rather than later. Meanwhile, God is calling out from Heaven:

I need you to understand My *First Coming* to begin with!
We have been satisfied with only one fragment of His work: that He came to save us from sin so He can eventually take us to Heaven.

The majority of Christians are stagnated in that truth and haven't been taught the fullness and the magnificence that Messiah came to do on Earth. The result is that they're living in terrible defeat with problems they have no business living in and, furthermore believing that the good things they are waiting for, will happen only when Jesus returns. As long as we continue to see everything in the far-off future, we will never feel challenged to possess today all the blessings, power, and the authority Jesus bought for us.

We can only receive from God what we believe He has granted us. It then becomes important to understand what He has done so that a misinterpretation of the Word does not rob us of our inheritance.

To belong to Jesus implies being a people different from the rest of the world not only in our ideology of salvation but also in the powerful manifestation of Who Jesus is in us.

Jesus came to manifest His Father, and this is our mission, too. As true sons and daughters of God we are here to manifest the Father in all His power and sovereignty. We will only have the faculty to beget sons and daughters of God according to the measure we reveal the Father through our lives.

Handing out salvation tracts is lovely, but it doesn't manifest the Life of the Father nor does it reproduce sons and daughters of the Spirit.

The world has to see in us a people who don't get sick, who lack nothing, but instead who give everything; people brimming with life and vigor even in their old age; a people who have the most extraordinary solutions to society's problems. A people who know how to use the power of God to change every circumstance, who know how to appease storms and bring rain during a drought; a people like there has never been time after time, throughout the many generations.

For this to happen we need to know the "Gospel of the Kingdom" and understand its significance to our lives.

2. JESUS CAME TO BRING THE KINGDOM OF HIS FATHER

Jesus came to establish a Kingdom, not to establish churches. The Church is the congregation of believers that form part of the King of kings' governmental system. A kingdom cannot be divided against itself.

The 40+ thousand Christian denominations that exist today have no power to change the world; only the unified Kingdom of God can achieve this. If we understand the true and powerful mission of our Messiah, we will be able to unite and transform our nations.

During His manifestation on Earth, Jesus constantly preached about the Kingdom of God as something nearby.

... and saying, 'The time is fulfilled, and the Kingdom of God is at hand. Repent ye and believe the Gospel.'

Mark 1:15

He commanded the preaching of the Gospel of the Kingdom and not the dispensation of Grace.

And as ye go, preach, saying, 'The Kingdom of Heaven is at hand.'
Heal the sick, cleanse the lepers, raise the dead, cast out devils. Freely ye have received; freely give.
Matthew 10:7-8

It's important to understand that Jesus came to bring the Kingdom of His Father and to prepare that first generation to enter in and govern together with Him. He came to give us spacious entry into the Kingdom not, when we die or for an uncertain future, but for the here and now.

The Gospel, which is the Good News, only makes sense to the extent that the work of the cross is effective for us while we are alive. Jesus did not take into His body our sins, our sicknesses, and our grief for us to enjoy this only after we die.

The Good News is that the cross defeated the devil and death so we could live in holiness, in health, in joy, in righteousness, and in prosperity while we are alive.

What sense does it make to preach to the poor and to the sick a future Kingdom without a solution to their current problems? Could we call it 'Good News'?

If the Kingdom is not in our midst, as many suppose, and postponed until the *second coming* of Christ, then the work of the cross, and the Good News of the Gospel are senseless.

Why would Jesus send us to preach something that could not be fulfilled until we got to Heaven? Why did He say that "the latter glory of this house would be greater than the former" unless this was going to be fulfilled? (The former house is the *Old Covenant;* the latter, the *New.*)

If He came to restore that which had been lost, that being the dominion God gave Adam to rule over the Earth, why did He say **'It is finished'** if we needed to wait more than 2000 years? Jesus came so that everything would return to be as His Father had created it at the beginning: God ruling from Heaven and man in fellowship with Him, ruling on Earth.

He came to unite Heaven and Earth once again reconciling them through the cross, not sometime in the future but from the moment of His death.

... and having made peace through the blood of His cross, by Him to reconcile all things unto Himself -- by Him, I say, whether they be things on earth or things in heaven.
Colossians 1:20

We can see from New Testament Scripture that is was clear to the apostles how God had returned to us our fellowship with Him, the dominion and the Kingdom.

*Therefore, **we receiving a Kingdom** which cannot be moved, let us have grace whereby we may serve God acceptably, with reverence and godly fear.*
Hebrews 12:28

Fear not, little flock, for it is your Father's good pleasure
to give you the Kingdom.   Luke 12:32

In this passage Jesus was encouraging them not to fear because He had come to establish the Kingdom, not for when they were already dead, but for whenever they felt they had a reason to fear.

Before the outpouring of the Holy Spirit, Jesus taught His apostles about the Kingdom. They needed to know how the Kingdom was going to be manifested and how they should reign by the Spirit. Why would He have talked about something that was to manifest itself in 2,000-plus years during the most important period of His ministry?

He wasn't talking to them about a 2000-year grace period, as some preach today He talked to them about The Kingdom He had come to establish.

To these also He showed Himself alive after His passion by many infallible proofs, being seen by them forty days, and speaking of the things pertaining to the Kingdom of God.
Acts 1:3

Jesus said *when seeking the Kingdom of God and its righteousness all these things would be added.* He then mentions the pertinent matters to our sustenance here on Earth.

Therefore take no thought, saying, 'What shall we eat?' or 'What shall we drink?' or 'Wherewith shall we be clothed?' (For after all these things do the Gentiles seek.) For your heavenly Father knoweth that ye have need of all these things. But seek ye first the Kingdom of God and His righteousness, and all these things shall be added unto you.   *Matthew 6:31-33*

He told the Pharisees and the Priests where and when His Kingdom would manifest itself:

Now when He was asked by the Pharisees when the kingdom of God would come, He answered them and said, "The kingdom of God does not come with observation; nor will they say, 'See here!' or 'See there!' For indeed, the kingdom of God is within you."   *Luke 17:20-21*

He referred to John the Baptist as the greatest of the Old Testament prophets and as the greatest among those who were born of women; however, He then pointed him out as the least in the Kingdom of God.

Verily I say unto you, among them that are born of women, there hath not risen a greater than John the Baptist; notwithstanding, he that is least in the Kingdom of Heaven is greater than he.
And from the days of John the Baptist until now, the Kingdom of Heaven suffereth violence, and the violent take it by force.   *Matthew 11:11-12*

Those born of the Spirit and water are greater than those born of women even if they were once a great prophet. **The Kingdom is not a place, it is a person, is Jesus Himself. To enter His Kingdom is to enter Jesus and He in us.** This makes us greater than those who were only anointed but were never born of God.

The Kingdom is for those who take it by force here on Earth. Jesus would not have used this verb if He were only referring to those who died and went to Heaven by faith and by grace.

The name of Jesus underwent a glory-to-glory transformation. He was born with the name *Jesus of Nazareth*, originally *Yeshua*. Upon being baptized, the anointing of the Father came upon Him and He became *Jesus the Christ or Messiah*, which means the *"Anointed of God."* But in ascending to the Throne of Glory and seating at the right hand of the Father, He was given a new name, a name that is above all names: **Yeshua the Lord.**

> *... that at the name of Jesus every knee should bow, of things in Heaven and things on earth and things under the earth,*
> *...and that every tongue should confess that Jesus Christ is Lord, to the glory of God the Father...*
> *Philippians 2:10-11*

In Timothy's first epistle, Paul refers to Jesus as "King of kings and Lord of lords."

> *.. .which He in His times shall show- He who is the blessed and only Potentate, the King of kings and Lord of lords,*
> *...*   *1 Timothy 6:15*

Paul does not transfer the lordship or the rulership of Jesus Christ to a time in the future, and nobody in the present-day Church has an issue with calling Him in this manner or believing that He is seated at the right hand of the Father in majesty.

Peter, on the day of Pentecost, acknowledges Him already in His Lordship:

"Therefore let all the house of Israel know assuredly that God has made this Jesus, whom you crucified, both Lord and Christ."   Acts 2:36

Now, if He is seated at the right hand of the Father and has already been crowned King of kings, why is it that many don't believe He reigns? They think He will only reign when He physically sits on the throne in earthly *Jerusalem* and meanwhile, what is He doing at the Father's right hand? Is he scratching His head waiting to reign someday and deliver us from our misery and our problems?

No king is ever crowned, nor does he sit on the throne, lest it be to exert his authority.

The truth is that Jesus is King of kings and Lord of lords, and He is reigning jointly with all who understand that they ARE HIS BODY. If the Head reigns, the body reigns jointly with it.

Salvation consists of acknowledging that He reigns as sovereign Lord.

*Because if you acknowledge and confess with your lips that **Jesus is Lord** and in your heart believe (adhere to, trust in, and rely on the truth) that God raised Him from the dead, you will be saved.*   Romans 10:9 AMP

He said "My Kingdom is not of this world." His Kingdom is of the Spirit, that is why no one can see the Kingdom except those who are born of water and of the Spirit. The devil doesn't care if we call Jesus "Lord" as long as we don't acknowledge Him in His ruling authority, seated at the right hand of the Father, ruling our lives and the nations. The truth is when we see Him in His Kingdom, our infirmities, problems and pains are gone. Therefore since all these things are under His feet, when we are ruling and reigning with Him they are also under ours.

The *Jerusalem* on Earth, its temple, and its history are but a shadow of the things that were to come when truth was manifested, and this was the *First Coming* of Messiah in the flesh.

For if He were on earth, *He should not be a priest, seeing that there are priests who offer gifts according to the law, and who serve unto the copy and shadow of heavenly things, as Moses was admonished by God when he was about to make the tabernacle. For, "See," saith He, 'that thou make all things according to the pattern shown to thee on the mount.' But now hath He obtained a more excellent ministry, by how much also He is the Mediator of a better covenant, which was established upon better promises.* Hebrews 8:4-6

The *Heavenly Jerusalem* reigns today and is made up of converted Jews and gentiles. God made ONE nation out of the two.

"But he who was of the bondwoman was born according to the flesh, but he of the freewoman was by promise." These things are an allegory representing the two covenants: The one is from

86

Mount Sinai, which engenders bondage; this is Hagar. The other is Isaac which is free.

> *For this Hagar is Mount Sinai in Arabia and answereth to Jerusalem as it is now, and is in bondage with her children.*
> *But the Jerusalem, which is above, is free, and is the mother of us all.*
> *Now we, brethren, as Isaac was, are the children of promise.*   *Galatians 4:23-26, 28*

Today many people and churches who are not living in the power of the Kingdom purchased for us at the price of the cross await the *Second Coming* for Jesus to bring them the Kingdom and heal their sickness and wipe every tear. Dear reader, He already did this during His *First Coming* and it will become clearer further on when we get to the understanding of the **New Jerusalem.**

The *Second Coming* is not related to being redeemed from the devil and his works. That is part of the first one.

The Kingdom of God is heavenly, not worldly; Jesus reigns, seated at the right hand of the Father from the *Jerusalem* above.

> *IF THEN you have been raised with Christ [to a new life, thus sharing His resurrection from the dead],* ***aim at and seek the [rich, eternal treasures] that are above,*** *where Christ is, seated at the right hand of God (which means ruling and reigning).*
>   *Colossians 3:1 AMP*
>   *(Emphasis added by the author)*

*And set your minds and keep them **set on what is above** (the higher things), **not on the things that are on the earth.***
For [as far as this world is concerned] you have died, and your [new, real] life is hidden with Christ in God.
Colossians 3:2-3 AMP

I want to make it clear that if Jesus is not reigning in His Kingdom, and if He is not yet seated on His Throne of Glory, then He has NOT been crowned as King of kings either, and this stance creates a gigantic conflict.

This stance leaves us in a limbo of uncertainty where nothing has happened between Christ's ascension and His coming in the clouds. Thinking that Jesus is not yet ruling in His Kingdom keeps people in a state of passivity and waiting, just holding until He comes back. At this moment in time the Church in general lacks authority, on one end we say "we are kings and priests," yet deep inside we consider it solely as a theological position but not a reality.

The majority of God's people do not know how to rule, how to take authority or how to change their circumstances because the Kingdom has been transferred to an uncertain future. To those who think this way, the Kingdom is only a hope but not a reality, and this is the reason the devil is winning most battles in their lives. If this state of limbo or waiting period is right, then the glorious Gospel of Jesus Christ is senseless in our lives. We live in the same pain, lack and infirmity as any non-convert, and the only thing we possess is our hope for when we die or when Christ returns.

If this is true, all the promises we previously read regarding the Kingdom make no sense either.

As I stated previously at the beginning of this chapter, we are living in perilous times where our preconceived ideas box us in and distort us so we are unable to see the glory of our Messiah as it was during His *First Coming.*

But if our Gospel be hid, it is hid to those who are lost, whose unbelieving minds the god of this world hath blinded, **lest the light of the glorious Gospel of Christ, who is the image of God, should shine unto them.**
2 Corinthians 4:3-4

Nowadays a gospel of grace and salvation is preached but the light of the gospel of the glory of Christ, the Lord of lords reigning in full power and authority continues veiled for those who live in disbelief, especially disbelief about the already present Kingdom and its power.

People are so step-by-step structured as to what has to happen before, during, and after the *Second Coming* of Jesus that the same thing that happened to the scribes and doctors of the Law could happen to them. If Jesus does not move according to their theologies and preconceived ideas, they will not see Him.

At this moment in time, there are hundreds of thousands of us living and experiencing the power and the majesty of the Kingdom of God. The Kingdom is not a far-away hope, but instead, it is a visible, palpable, and demonstrative reality.

The *First Coming* of Messiah is ABSOLUTELY POWERFUL and we have to understand and value everything that was paid for us at the cross of Calvary to give us access to the new life in the Kingdom of God.

I invite you to be brave and de-structure yourself to find that neutral and humble position so the heavens may open further over your life and His Holy Spirit announce what He is saying to you.

8 GOD'S TABERNACLE WITH MAN AND THE *NEW JERUSALEM*

1. THE TABERNACLE OF FLESH

We have already analyzed our *first and second basic themes:* The new Heaven and new Earth and the works of Messiah. We will now touch on *the third basic theme:* God's Tabernacle with men. It's important to analyze them and to be able to understand the different themes in the *Book of Revelation* to develop a suitable eschatology If this theme is made clear to us, many of the confusing puzzle pieces will fall into place.

History establishes that the physical temple in *Jerusalem* was destroyed in the year 70 A.D. Through his death and resurrection, Jesus was to establish a new tabernacle in the believers: the temple of God in the Spirit, which was to replace the one made of stone.

Jesus answered and said unto them, 'Destroy this temple, and in three days I will raise it up.' John 2:19

What? Know ye not that your body is the temple of the Holy Ghost which is in you and which ye have from God, and that ye are not your own ? 1 Corinthians 6:19

*Now therefore, ye are strangers and foreigners no more, but **fellow citizens** with the saints, and of the household of God. Ye are built upon the foundation of the apostles and prophets, Jesus Christ Himself being the chief cornerstone, in whom all the building, fitly framed together, groweth unto a **holy temple** in the Lord, in Whom ye also are built together for a habitation of God **through the Spirit.***

Ephesians 2:19-22

These passages of Scripture are the fulfillment of the words spoken by the prophet Ezekiel:

*Moreover I will make a covenant of peace with them. It shall be an **everlasting covenant** with them. And I will place them, and multiply them, and will set My sanctuary in the midst of them for evermore. **My tabernacle also shall be with them. Yea, I will be their God, and they shall be My people.** And the heathen shall know that I, the LORD, do sanctify Israel, when My sanctuary shall be in the midst of them for evermore.*

Ezekiel 37:26-27

All theologies agree that this prophecy is fulfilled with Christ's First Coming when the Lord makes His abode in us, His children.

*Jesus answered and said unto him, 'If a man loves Me, he will keep My words; and My Father will love him, and We will come unto him and **make Our abode with him.'***

John 14:23

The Holy Spirit living in us, makes it possible for the Father and the Son to make their abode in our spirit, which God transforms into the new ark where He establishes His presence. These theologies are all in agreement that this is not for the future but for us today. However, when we read this same scripture in the Book of Revelation, we no longer believe this is for today but for the future. It's in this confusion where the devil steals from us the power to reign with Christ.

*And I, John, saw the holy city, New Jerusalem, coming down from God out of Heaven, prepared as a bride adorned for her husband. And I heard a great voice out of Heaven, saying, **'Behold, the tabernacle of God is with men, and He will dwell with them; and they shall be His people, and God Himself shall be with them and be their God.'***

Revelation 21:2-3

This confusion occurs because we have deeply rooted in our minds and in our theologies how Revelation 21 HAS TO HAPPEN after the destruction of the Earth, that we are unable to see how this passage of Scripture is exactly the same as Ezekiel's prophecy regarding Christ's First Coming. The *Book of Revelation* is not an isolated revelation, it is coherent with it is confirmed by the Old Testament that confirms it.

God is not going to establish His tabernacle in the midst of men in the future,; He already did it. The Church is His temple,; He legitimately abides in the believers. **To think that He has not made His tabernacle in us is to deny the very heart of the Gospel.**

Therefore, if this is a fundamental truth, it will guide me to correctly interpret the rest of Chapter 21. The second concept,

93

which gives me the absolute certainty that this passage refers to something that already happened is this:

And He said unto me, 'It is done! I am Alpha and Omega, the beginning and the end. I will give unto him that is thirsty of the fountain of the Water of Life freely.'

Revelation 21:6

These are the same words Jesus uttered before dying. When He said, **"It is finished,"** He clearly made it known that His redemptive work was done; that the Ancient Covenant culminated at that moment, giving way to the New.

We need to understand that when Jesus spoke those words from the cross, he did not yet live in the heart of any believer. The right to live within us had been lawfully purchased, but it was not manifested until the day of Pentecost.

Additionally, in this scripture from the **Book of Revelation,** Jesus calls us to drink from the fountain of life, which is clearly a call to salvation, as He told the Samaritan woman at the well. He was speaking to a people living in a very dry land under the rulership of death and who needed to drink of Jesus.

This obviously doesn't make sense if the Earth was already destroyed, the saved are in Heaven and the lost are in hell, as it may be interpreted if we read the **Book of Revelation** in chronological order it was assumed to be put together in the fourth century.

I quickly understood how this refers to a message needed to be conveyed in order to bring hope to people who still remain under the yoke of sin and of death.

94

Keeping these principles in mind, we are going to analyze the rest of Revelation chapter 21.

a) Chapter 21 of the Book of Revelation

This is one of the most important chapters for our time and it's a true legacy God left for us. The next two basic themes we are analyzing, *the tabernacle of God* with men and *the New Jerusalem,* are vital to our walk with Christ and our understanding of the structure and the function of the Church in our day. Both are found in this passage; therefore, understanding it will clear up much of what is confusing.

The chapter begins with the declaration that "all things have been made new.." From the moment He sits on His throne at the right hand of the Father after His ascension marks the beginning of the Age of Messiah. Jesus has redeemed Heaven and Earth and an *Age of Light* has now begun.

And I saw a new heaven and a new earth, for the first heaven and the first earth had passed away, and there was no more sea.　　　　　　*Revelation 21:1*

The 'sea' in this Scripture is does not refer to the beautiful ocean God created, but to one of the three different types of seas in The *Book of Revelation,* a region of death.

(1) The Sea of God
nd I saw, as it were, a sea of glass mingled with fire, and them that had gotten the victory over the beast, and over his image, and over his mark, and over the number of his

name, standing on the sea of glass and having the harps of God.   *Revelation 15:2*

(2) The Earthly sea, which are the oceans

(3) The Sea, which is a region of death found under the oceans.

And the sea gave up the dead which were in it; and death and hell delivered up the dead which were in them; and they were judged every man according to their works.

Revelation 20:13

Note how the "sea" gives up its dead here. If these were the oceans, and it's alluding to those who drowned in it, then the passage would say, *"The sea gave up its dead and the land its deceased."* But it doesn't say that. It talks about three spiritual regions from where death rules: the Sea (also called the Abyss), Death, and Hades.

This place of death is also the one that sustains Babylon, the great harlot. The angel who decrees its judgment casts a millstone into the region of death, which sustains this spiritual structure. This region is over many peoples and nations.

*Then a mighty angel took up a stone like a great millstone, and cast it into **the sea,** saying, "Thus with violence shall that great city Babylon be thrown down, and shall be found no more at all."*

Revelation 18:21

*And I stood upon the **sand of the sea.** And I saw a beast rise up **out of the sea,** having seven heads and ten horns,* *and upon his horns ten crowns, and upon his heads the name of blasphemy.* Revelation 13:1

The beast mentioned in Revelation 13 arises from this region of death. This region of death keeps many nations captive and annihilates people's spiritual lives.

And he saith unto me, "The waters which thou sawest, where the whore sitteth, are peoples and multitudes, and nations and tongues. Revelation 17:15

2. THE NEW JERUSALEM

Beginning in verse 2 of Chapter 21 we see another topic surfacing which is clearly tied to God's tabernacle with man called the *New Jerusalem*. This is also our fourth basic theme of interpretation.

Throughout the Pauline epistles we see how the topic of the *Heavenly Jerusalem* is one of the names God uses to refer to His Church. The physical *Jerusalem* was the place where God abided during the Old Covenant. And the Jerusalem from above, the Heavenly One, are us the believers, Jews as well as Gentiles.

*For this Hagar is Mount Sinai in Arabia and answereth to **Jerusalem** as it is now, and is in bondage with her children. But the **Jerusalem** which is above is free, and is the mother of us all.* Galatians 4:25-26

*But ye have come unto Mount Zion and unto the city of the living God, the **heavenly Jerusalem,** and to an innumerable company of angels...* Hebrews 12:22

We clearly see how in these two passages the Church born of the Spirit is the *Heavenly Jerusalem;* we are the temple of God, the heavenly city.

Jesus has already established the heavenly city in our midst, and He is already the tree of life giving life to His Body as the vine does to the branches.

The heavenly city is our design as a glorious Church. The city is God's tabernacle with man. If the city were for the future, then, in actuality, we are not God's temple either.

Do you realize how important it is to understand this topic?

And I, John, saw the holy city, New Jerusalem, coming down from God out of Heaven, prepared as a bride adorned for her husband.

*And I heard a great voice out of Heaven, saying, "Behold, **the tabernacle of God is with men,** and He will dwell with them; and they shall be His people, and God Himself shall be with them and be their God."*

Revelation 21:2-3

As of this moment, John was quoting chapter 60 of Isaiah. Remember what Jesus said about the fulfillment of these prophecies: that everything concerning Him in the Torah, the Prophets, and the Psalms had already been fulfilled (Luke 24:44).

Violence shall no more be heard in thy land, wasting nor destruction within thy borders; but thou shalt

call thy walls Salvation and thy gates Praise.
The sun shall be no more thy light by day, neither for brightness shall the moon give light unto thee; but the LORD shall be unto thee an everlasting light, and thy God thy glory. Thy sun shall no more go down, neither shall thy moon withdraw itself; for the LORD shall be thine everlasting light, and **the days of thy mourning shall be ended.** *Thy people also shall be all righteous; they shall inherit the land forever, the branch of My planting, the work of My hands, that I may be glorified.*
Isaiah 60:18-21

To those of us who don't live the reality of the invisible Kingdom of the Spirit, these prophecies are incomprehensible. But to those who have united to Jesus in one Spirit, to the spouse of the Lamb, this is daily living. This same passage in Isaiah begins with the announcement of the work of Messiah, which all of us acknowledge is for our days.

Arise, shine, for **thy light is come, and the glory of the LORD is risen upon thee.**
For behold, the darkness shall cover the earth and gross darkness the people; but the LORD shall arise upon thee, and His glory shall be seen upon thee.
And the Gentiles shall come to thy light, and kings to the brightness of thy rising. *Isaiah 60:1-3*

This is the same light that shines full of glory in the heavenly city who is the Church. He is our only Light that illuminates our understanding.

In the Old Covenant, the land was full of thick dark clouds and deep darkness covered the nations, but when Messiah overcame He bequeathed to us His Light to illuminate the whole world with it.

Isaiah, as well as the **Book of Revelation,** talks about the glorious Church not as one in the future but in the here and now, a Church in the Spirit that believes in God.

Therefore thy gates shall be open continually; they shall not be shut day nor night, that men may bring unto thee the wealth of the Gentiles, and that their kings may be brought.   *Isaiah 60:11*

It's the Church who has those gates continually open for all who want to freely drink of the *waters of life.* But this is the Church seen from the heavens, the Church that has entered in to possess the Kingdom. These are not those who attend a Christian church and say "Lord, Lord."

Everybody may come in to our churches and listen to the Word, but not everybody can enter the Kingdom - only those who wash their clothes with the blood of the Lamb, depart from sin and iniquity, and take the Kingdom truths by force.

But the fearful, and unbelieving, and the abominable, and murderers, and whoremongers, and sorcerers, and idolaters, and all liars, shall have their part in the lake which burneth with fire and brimstone, which is the second death.
And there came unto me one of the seven angels, who

100

had the seven vials full of the seven last plagues, and talked with me, saying, 'Come hither; I will how thee the bride, the Lamb's wife.'

And he carried me away in the spirit to a great and high mountain, and showed me that great city, the Holy Jerusalem, descending out of Heaven from God, having the glory of God. And her light was like unto a stone most precious, even like a jasper stone, clear as crystal.

Revelation 21:8-11

These verses are analogous to those we just saw in Isaiah 60. John is talking here about God's designs descending from Heaven. Many people are unable to relate the word *Heaven* to their daily living because they see it as a place where they will be in the future, alien to their earthly reality.

To Jesus, Heaven and Earth are united in Him. He lived in the heavens and on Earth at the same time He moved in both dimensions simultaneously.

*If I have told you earthly things and ye believe not, how shall ye believe if I tell you of heavenly things? And **no man hath ascended up to Heaven, but He that came down from Heaven, even the Son of Man who is in Heaven.*** *John 3:12-13*

Jesus spoke this long before His ascension to Heaven. He said He went up and came down and that He was in Heaven. The truth is that this is the only authentic way of living in the Kingdom. Jesus opened the way to the heavens so we could boldly come before His Throne of Grace. Living in the revelation that John lived in is the commonplace realm to the children of God. In Jesus, Heaven and Earth have been united,; those who are genuinely in Jesus have access to the heavens just as Jesus had it when He was on Earth.

...having made known to us the mystery of His will, according to His good pleasure which He purposed in Himself,

*...that in the dispensation of the fullness of the times He might gather together in one all things in Christ, **both which are in heaven and which are on earth—in Him.*** Ephesians 1:9-10

Thousands of people are taken up continually to see and experience Heaven's dimensions. If this is still not a reality for you, maybe it's because you never considered the possibility. Dare to believe and take the Kingdom by force for your life!

Religion views Heaven as something up high and far away, but Jesus brought it to Earth so we could enjoy it while we are still alive here on Earth.

Jesus prepared the heavenly city for us so wherever He's at, that we may also be.

*In My Father's house are many mansions; if it were not so, I would have told you. I go to prepare a place for you. And if I go and prepare a place for you, I will come again and receive you unto Myself, **that where I am, there ye may be also.*** John 14:2-3

If Jesus is in us and we are in Him, then our spiritual house is also in our midst.

> *For we know that if our earthly house, this tabernacle, were dissolved, we have a building of God, a house not made with hands, eternal in the heavens.*
> *For in this we groan, **earnestly desiring to be clothed about with our house which is from Heaven,** that, being so clothed, we shall not be found naked. For we that are in this tabernacle do groan, being burdened, not because we would be unclothed, but clothed about, **that mortality might be swallowed up by life.***
>
> *2 Corinthians 5:1-4*

We see in this passage how our spiritual house is our true clothing. Paul groans to be clothed with that house. It doesn't come to him by the work of grace; he has to take it by force through prayer and untold groans. The wonderful result of being clothed in our heavenly clothing is that our mortality is swallowed up by life.

God's Tabernacle is Jesus Himself being formed in us. He is the Kingdom and He is also the city that descends from Heaven.

When I understand this and pursue it untill it becomes a reality in my life, all the mortality of this world cannot touch me.

This is not a manner of speaking or a manner of interpreting Scripture, it's the reality many of us are already living.

The Father as well as the Son manifest themselves in our lives through that heavenly clothing.

> ... *"At that day ye shall know that I am in My Father, and you in Me, and I in you.*
> *He that hath My commandments and keepeth them, he it is that loveth Me; and he that loveth Me shall be loved by My Father, and I will love him and* **will manifest Myself to him."**
> *Judas (not Iscariot) said unto Him,* **"Lord, how is it that Thou wilt manifest Thyself unto us, and not unto the world?"**
> *Jesus answered and said unto him, "If a man love Me, he will keep My words; and My Father will love him, and We will come unto him and* **make Our abode with him."**
>
> *John 14:20-23*

When God manifests Himself by making His abode with us, then we learn how we have been conceived. We no longer see ourselves in our problems and weaknesses, but as the powerful sons and daughters of God full of the glory He already gave us to rule on Earth.

> *If ye then be risen with Christ, seek those things which are above, where Christ sitteth at the right hand of God. Set your affection on things above, not on things on the earth.*
> *For ye are dead, and your life is hid with Christ in God.*
> *When Christ, who is our life, shall appear, then shall ye also appear with Him in glory.* *Colossians 3:1-4*

Let's go back to the passage in Revelation 21:

And the city had no need of the sun, neither of the moon to shine in it; for the glory of God gave it light, and the Lamb is the light thereof.   *Revelation 21:23*

Jesus is the light that illuminates our temple. While on Earth, He took three of His disciples to the top of the mountain to show them He Himself was the kingdom, the power and the glory. Moses and Elijah appeared to represent the Law and the Prophets as witnesses to the glory of God. Jesus shone much more than the noonday sun showing them the *Heavenly Jerusalem* described in the **Book of Revelation.**

The heavenly city is the Body of Jesus composed of living stones who are all the believers in their individual beauty and characteristics. It has the brightness of God on its walls and its make-up is cubed, the same way as the Holy of Holies because the living God dwells therein. The tree of Life and the river of life are in its center, and both are Jesus, Who is the eternal life and the water that quickens all who drink it. It's from within us that the fountain of life springs forth producing the *River of God.*

But whosoever drinketh of the water that I shall give him shall never thirst; but the water that I shall give him shall be in him a well of water springing up into everlasting life.
John 4:14

He who understand what it means to be the temple of God knows that his/her spirit is the very altar from where the waters of life flow, and he/she does not allow any contamination to enter.

These people don't have to ask God to take them to the Holy of Holies as if it were a place separated from them, they live; breathes and feed from it.

Its design is not a pyramid with a man at the summit and the rest underneath, but it's a cube representing the united Body in harmony, with ONE single head, Who is Christ. Today we have many pyramids as the Church structure, but God has already started a marvelous work in many of them, uniting them by the Spirit to form the true design by which He can rule entire cities and nations. **The design of the Church is a city,** not a whole lot of denominations divided one from another.

Very soon we will see thousands of churches filled with the knowledge of God, transforming the pyramidal system into a City-Church, and the glory of God will overflow them.

Its foundation is the apostolic government of Christ. These are apostles and prophets who are not seeking to be seen but instead, they are covered by precious stones, which are their spiritual disciples raised up by pastors, teachers and evangelists to shine forth as the fruit of their true apostleship.

The doors are 12 pearls, because they open into the city, is which is the Kingdom of God, which is also the pearl of great price. Christ himself is the pearl, His government and His principles symbolized by the number 12.

A suffering oyster makes a pearl when either sand or a tiny pebble gets inside it. This speaks of Jesus, "The Rock," dressed up in glory by through His sufferings. It is the redemptive work of Jesus at the cross that gives us access to the eternal city.

The mission of the city (which is the unity of Christ and His wife) is to shine brightly and carry the glory of God to the nations. It's the light that shines over Mount Zion for the illumination of the knowledge of God. The city is careful that no uncleanliness enters her, and she opens her door to bring in those who are thirsty for the Lord.

She is not divided, nor is there competition amongst her own members, but she is united at its joints and is being built up as a spiritual building.

And are built upon the foundation of the apostles and prophets, Jesus Christ himself being the chief corner stone; **In whom all the building fitly framed together groweth unto an holy temple in the Lord:** *In whom ye also are builded together for an habitation of God through the Spirit.* Ephesians 2:20-22

The city descends from Heaven because such are the designs of God for His Church, who is His spouse. We marry the Lamb in the dimensions of the Spirit.

9   THE LAMB'S SPOUSE

T his is one of the most important subjects the Holy Spirit wants us to understand, since it's fundamental to know what has been granted to us on God's behalf. This is also our *fifth basic theme* of interpretation, which will set into place many loose pieces of the *Book of Revelation* puzzle.

Marriage is consummated when a man and woman become one flesh in intimacy, when she becomes flesh of his flesh, bone of his bones; the apostle Paul distinctly writes about this.

> *For the husband is head of the wife as Christ is the Head of the church, Himself the Savior of* ***[His] body.***
> *Ephesians 5:23 AMP*

> *For no man ever hated his own flesh, but nourishes and carefully protects and cherishes it, as Christ does the church,*
> *Because we are members (parts) of* ***His body.***
> *For this reason a man shall leave his father and his mother and shall be joined to his wife, and the two shall become one flesh.*

This mystery is very great, but I speak concerning [the relation of] Christ and the church.
Ephesians 5:29-32

But he that is joined unto the Lord is one spirit with Him.
1 Corinthians 6:17

These passages provides evidence beyond a doubt that to be the Body of Christ, we necessarily have to be joined to Him as His wife.

When a man and a woman marry they become one flesh. When we marry Jesus we become ONE SPIRIT with Him. When He said: **"It is finished,"** He meant that the work was done. He completely and absolutely washed us by His blood. There are no more spots or wrinkles in us because of His blood; we are clean as snow. **This is the work of grace.**

Understanding this makes a complete difference. If I am only Christ's bride waiting to marry Him in the future, then I'm still not His Body. The bride has no legal access to anything that belongs to the bridegroom, but once married, she has access to everything. Only the wife has the King's checkbook and has open doors for intimacy with Him; before the weedings the bride has only a hope.

This is a matter of central importance, because while we continue waiting for the wedding feast of the Lamb at some uncertain time in the future, we don't have access to anything, and this is where the devil robs us of the power, the riches, and our entry into the King's chambers.

Apostle John Eckhardt writes in his book, *Behold I come quickly:*

"The eschatological wedding is connected to the fall of Babylon. Both occurred at the end of the age. The whore (covenant breaking and apostate Israel) is judged and a new marriage (new covenant Church[12]) is consummated."

"The eschatological wedding is the fulfillment of God's promise to Israel of being betrothed in righteousness (Hosea 2:19-20). This betrothal was through Christ and the New Covenant. The New Covenant Church in the first century consisted of both Jews and Gentiles. The invitation to the marriage was given in the first century, and all things were made ready then (Matt 22:1-4). Some have tried to put the wedding at the end of the Christian age instead of the end of the Jewish age."

"The parable of the ten virgins (Matt 25) reflects the betrothal of Christ and His Church. The Lord left to prepare a place for His bride, and would return to take her to the bridal chamber. The five virgins were those prepared for his return, and the five foolish represented those unprepared. Oil represents the anointing and living by the Holy Spirit."

"The time of betrothal would not last for thousands

---

[12] Note from the author: The new covenant Church includes Israel and gentiles. From the two people He made one. God will never forsake Israel, nor has replaced it with the Church, however, the only way of salvation is through Jesus, the Messiah.

I belive God will still move mightly in the Israel of today, bringing a major harvest of His people into His Father's Kingdom.

of years. The betrothal would last for a generation. The marriage of the Lamb would occur shortly (Rev 1:1,3; 19:7-9). John the Baptist rejoiced because he Heard the bridegroom's voice (John 3:29). This again has a first century application. Jesus the Bridegroom had appeared and began calling His church to the marriage."

"The betrothal was prophesied by Hosea (Hosea 2:19-20). Israel's unfaithfulness to the old covenant, would result in a new covenant a new betrothal. The parable of the ten virgins reflects the Jewish wedding custom of Jesus day. The groom would be delayed while he prepared a dwelling for his bride at his father's house. The groom returns for his bride once the dwelling is finished (John 14:1-3). The bride and groom then go in procession to the groom's father's house for the marriage feast.

And I heard as it were the voice of a great multitude, and as the voice of many waters, and as the voice of mighty thundering, saying, Alleluia: for the Lord God omnipotent reigneth. Let us be glad and rejoice, and give honour to him: for the marriage of the Lamb is come, and his wife hath made herself ready."

Revelation 19:6-7

"The reign of God had come and was manifested through the judgments upon Babylon. The saints are glad and rejoice because the marriage has arrived and the saints now receive the blessings of the consummated kingdom. This is what the early Church was taught by the apostles to expect and receive in their lifetime."[13]

*In my Father's house are many mansions: if it were not so, I would have told you. I go to prepare a place for you. And if I go and prepare a place for you, I will come again, and receive you unto myself; **that where I am, there ye may be also.*** John 14:2-3

Jesus is in the heart of the believers and we are in Him.

1. THE CONSUMMATION OF THE WEDDINGS OF THE LAMB
REVELATION 19

The Church, the Body of Christ, is already His wife. What then, is the marriage supper in the *Book of Revelation,* and how is this wedding manifested in our lives?

As we have been studying, this is a living book and a kingdom manual thatqualifies us to rule with Christ. Upon reading Chapter 19 as well as 21, it becomes clear to us that this legacy from John is not chronological.

The first thing I want you to notice is that in this passage known as "the wedding supper of the Lamb" no marriage ceremony is mentioned, and the groom is nowhere to be found.

It is important to remember that the titles assigned to the chapters in the Bible are not of divine inspiration. They were put there along with the division of chapters and verse numbers to

---

[13] Behold I come quickly, John Eckhardt. pgs 161 y 162

113

help the readers of Scripture. Unfortunately, as we read the titles in the *Book of Revelation* they divert us from the true meaning and lock us into the mindset of those who drafted them.

Therefore, let us forget the titles and focus on the principles of understanding that we are developing.

Let us be glad and rejoice and give honor to Him, for the marriage of the Lamb is come, and His wife hath made herself ready."
And to her was granted that she should be arrayed in fine linen, clean and white; for the fine linen is the righteousness of saints.
*And he said unto me, "Write: `Blessed are they **that are called unto the marriage supper of the Lamb.'**" And he said unto me, "These are the true sayings of God."*
*And I fell at his feet to worship him. But he said unto me, "See that thou do it not! I am thy fellow servant and one of thy brethren, who hold to the testimony of Jesus. Worship God! For **the testimony of Jesus is the spirit of prophecy."***   *Revelation 19:7-10*

I emphasized in bold letters the two key parts to understand what God is attempting to tell us. The first thing He wants to show us is the realm in which the union of His Spirit with ours occurs, and secondly, how this happens.

Where does it happen? The place is *in God's prophetic dimension.*

John falls to his feet before the angel because of the impressive visions and revelations he is receiving from God. However, the angel clears it up for him to worship God because everything he is seeing and experiencing is the Spirit of prophecy, which is the testimony of Jesus. In other words, what the angel of the Lord is saying is, "Everything you are seeing and experiencing is Jesus Himself, it is the revelation of everything Jesus came to do." The Spirit of prophecy is the realm where you get to know Him in His fullness because the dimension of the Spirit is Jesus Himself. Jesus and the heavens are one, and you have to be immersed in Him to experience it.

The blessing is in partaking of the Lord's Supper, because when you eat and drink of His blood, His Spirit and His life marry you.

To eat and to drink of Him opens our understanding and transfers us to the dimension where He reigns.[14]

The Lord's supper is to live in Him and to participate in the glory of His judgments over every ungodliness, dining with Him is delighting ourselves in His righteousness.

Do ye not know that the saints shall judge the world? And if the world shall be judged by you, are ye unworthy to judge the smallest matters?
Know ye not that we shall judge angels? How much more,   *1 Corinthians 6:2-3*

When we dine with Him, His Spirit fuses with ours, and the heavens open up for us to understand and to know Christ as

---

[14] You can find the depth of this topic througout my book Eat of my flesh and drink of My Blood. By Ana Méndez Ferrell. AMF Inc.

King, Ruler and **Judge of the universe.**

Jesus unites to that true believer who has left their life of sin to subject themselves to the Lordship of their spouse in Heaven. Many of the church attendees nowadays are still in the engagement stage but they have not married yet. These people have entered into a covenant of salvation and are undergoing a process of regeneration. Jesus considers these as part of Him, but they cannot enjoy the privileges of the wife until their conversion and their surrender to God is a total one. To achieve this, it is necessary to be an overcomer.

> *Behold, I stand at the door and knock. If anyone hears My voice and opens the door, I will come in to him and dine with him, and he with Me. To him who overcomes I will grant to sit with Me on My throne, as I also overcame and sat down with My Father on His throne.*
>
> *Revelation 3:20-21*

To rule means to bring justice to an offended party and judgment to the ungodly; it is also the administration of all of Earth and Heaven's resources.

When our spirit merges with God's in the marriage of the Spirit, then Heaven's dimensions open up to us and we are granted the faculty to fight and to judge with Him. That is why after the wedding supper of the Lamb John sees the heavens open and Jesus on His white horse.

> *And I saw **Heaven opened,** and behold, a white horse; and He that sat upon him was called Faithful and True,*

and in righteousness He doth judge and make war.

His eyes were as a flame of fire, and on His head were many crowns; and He had a name written that no man knew, but He Himself.

And He was clothed with a vesture dipped in blood, and His name is called, THE WORD OF GOD.

And the armies which were in Heaven, clothed in fine linen white and clean, followed Him upon white horses.

And out of His mouth goeth a sharp sword with which He shall smite the nations, and He shall rule them with a rod of iron; and He treadeth the wine press of the fierceness and wrath of Almighty God.

And He hath on His vesture and on His thigh a name written: KING OF KINGS, AND LORD OF LORDS.

And I saw an angel standing in the sun, and he cried with a loud voice, saying to all the fowls that fly in the midst of heaven, "Come and gather yourselves together unto the supper of the great God.

Revelation 19:11-17

Jesus will not receive the name "The Word of God" or the title of His reign sometime in the future. He has already been crowned King of kings and Lord of lords, and He is already on Earth fighting our battles and establishing His justice over the Earth. There are individual judgments over men and there are judgments over cities and nations. The judgments of God will not be all at once in one single day. God has been judging the nations forever, and this becomes obvious throughout history.

When in Scripture it talks about horses ridden by men it symbolizes the strength and pride of men. In this case Jesus rides the horse, which speaks about the authority and the power He has given to His spouse.

Jesus in His white horse represents the union of His Spirit with ours. We are the white horse, redeemed and sanctified, which He can direct with the reins of His wisdom to execute justice along with Him.

*...for the LORD of hosts hath visited his flock the house of Judah, and **hath made them as his goodly horse in the battle.*** Zechariach 10:3b KJV

And after these things I heard a great voice of a multitude of people in Heaven, saying, "Alleluia! Salvation and glory and honor and power, unto the Lord our God, for true and righteous are His judgments: He hath judged the great whore who corrupted the earth with her fornication, and hath avenged the blood of His servants at her hand."
And again they said, "Alleluia!" And her smoke rose up for ever and ever.
And the four and twenty elders and the four living beings fell down and worshiped God who sat on the throne, saying, "Amen! Alleluia!"
And a voice came out of the throne, saying, "Praise our God, all ye His servants, and ye that fear Him, both small and great."
*And I heard, as it were, the voice of a great multitude, and the voice of many waters, and the voice of mighty thunderings, saying, **"Alleluia! For the Lord God Omnipotent reigneth."*** Revelation 19:1-6

The Church, who is His wife, knows how to legislate in the heavens to bring justice and judgment to Earth. It's an intercessory Church who cries out for Justice and also for salvation and mercy. She knows the beating of the Father's heart and joins Him so His judgments are carried out. She rejoices in knowing Him as sovereign King and righteous Judge. She rides with Him in battle to establish His Kingdom upon the Earth.

One of the things God is restoring in our lifetime is the establishment of His system of justice over the Earth. Every kingdom needs to have a supreme court of justice, and God also has one indeed. I will talk about this when we study the 24 elders of the *Book of Revelation.*

10   *Babylon, The Great Harlot*

1. TRAINED TO TEAR DOWN *BABYLON*

F rom the onset of His message in the *Book of Revelation,* Jesus is directing the prophecy into a climax, which is the judgment of *Babylon* - the Great Harlot - and of the corrupt systems of this world. To do this He has to refine the Church with the necessary enlightenment and tools to confront *Babylon* and subject her.

The first century Church was living under the conditions narrated in the seven letters of Revelation 2-3, which were designed to encourage and prepare them for the judgment that was to come between the years 66 and 70 A.D. (*See instrument 2*). However, their living and eternal content is part of our divine Kingdom manual.

Every judgment of God is just, and those who will be assigned to judge have to be purged from every *Babylonian* alliance and practice so they are not judged jointly with her.

And I saw thrones and they that sat upon them, and judgment was given unto them. Revelation 20:4

Do ye not know that the saints shall judge the world? And if the world shall be judged by you, are ye unworthy to judge the smallest matters? Know ye not that we shall judge angels? How much more, things that pertain to this life? 1 Corinthians 6:2-3

2. PATMOS, THIRD VISION

I found myself at the place of the doors inside God's heart when a man dressed in white garments appeared with me holding a little book in one of his hands and a key chain with many keys in the other. I asked who he was and why had he come, and he answered me, "I am one of the prophets of the Most High and I have been given the keys to open the prophecy. Jesus is the Spirit of Prophecy, and many Words have been closed up, and it has been granted us as prophets to open them." He then opened the little book and handed me a key. When I touched his hand to take it, a very bright light lit up my eyes as if they had their own light, and suddenly we where transported to desert plain in the midst of which was a very prosperous city. Although we were at a distance, we could see what was happening inside in full detail.

The city had a grotesque and abominable queen living in her palace with her son, and both had cast hexes and spells to ally themselves with the powers of the kingdom of darkness. The greater principalities gave them strength to extend their empire. Kings and peoples from the four corners of the Earth would come to them; big and small were entered into covenant and made to drink from a chalice that would inebriate them and have them believe their lies.

Upon drinking it, they were immediately surrounded by shadows that would speak to them while covering their eyes and ears. They laughed and felt happy because of the beverage that affected their reasoning and gave them great dreams, visions, and strength.

Their empire filled the whole Earth, and men would bring their wickedness as a tribute to them by doing this. Their empire became progressively enlarged and made more powerful. Then an opening above the city appeared as what seemed to be a different heaven from the one we were in; it was like a black hole, and it was horrendous.

In an instant, the prophet and I were there. This place was the same city but seen in another form. It no longer had the splendor and prosperity of the former one. It had turned into an enormous building in the shape of a dark and sinister pyramid; there were birds of prey and ravens everywhere. Inside and out there were prisons filled with millions of persons. The city had what looked like tentacles and highways that that came out of it and reached thousands of cities arranged in a similar fashion. These were the spiritual cities of deep darkness that are above each of Earth's metropolises.

Both above and below the city there were several dimensional planes. Some would sink to a horrid depth, and others appeared to be different levels above.

I asked the prophet what those places were and where we were. He told me, "This is the abominable city, the great harlot that has held the nations and the peoples captive. She captivates them through commerce, religion and politics." He then added, "Here the dimensions of the spirit are not like those on Earth where only one apparently solid existential plane in three dimensions is visible. There are many more dimensions here, like the ones you saw in Heaven, the multiple dimensions of the Most High."

There were seven high mountains around the city, which were reflected in each of the different planes, like when you put one mirror in front of another. The roadways joined the mountains of the great city and served as supply routes from the seas, from hell, from sinfull men, and from the moon, the sun, and the constelations.

We entered through the city gates, which were cluttered with masonic and witchcraft symbols. There was a curtain at the entrance made of something like a liquid cloud; everyone who entered had to go through it. I saw millions of persons cross it. They came through in chains and in yokes. Others came so burdened by demons they could barely walk. As they cross, an aqueous, imperceptible mask that affected their whole reality came over them and covered their faces. The mask enabled them to feel good and to view the abominable as precious. They called evil good and good evil, yet they were nothing more than robots in a system.

Upon seeing this, I was afraid to cross over, but the prophet took one of his keys and extended it in front of the watery door that opened without touching us. I then noticed that a magnificent covering of light surrounded us. The prophet told me, "Fear not for those who have the Spirit of Prophecy can cross through here without being touched. Jesus is the Truth and he who walks in it, walks in His Light."

After crossing, we entered a deep murk. Inside was a city with streets and public squares, but all over there were prisons at differing levels of depth and darkness. We walked a long way untill we reached an avenue that led to one of the mountains. The name of this mountain was *Religion*, and the avenue was *Jezebel*. An enormous demon was guarding it and directing the people towards the mountain. There were many dining areas along the avenue where people delighted themselves in getting fat. Some never reached the mountain; instead, they fell into the abyss where they continued getting fat and worshipped a horrible demon whose appearance was like that of a toad whose skin overflowed with food of all sorts. It was the spirit of *gluttony* that served the queen prostitute next to the other two toads. One was *Mammon*, the god of riches, and the other was *Pharmakeia*, the goddess of sorcery.

When we got to the mountain, I was jolted by the sharp resemblance it had to the mountain of God that I had seen in His glory, full of small mountains where all of them comprised Jesus.

The mountain here was a great pyramid and full of small pyramids. Each one had the name of a kingdom, and a man was exalted at the summit. The pyramid was made of partition walls that formed prisons, all of which were grounded from a dark substance full of lettering. All of the prisons were conformed to the image of the man at the summit, and they all wore masks from the water cloud. They were continuously fed contaminated food, but they perceived it as delicious due to the mask and because they yearned to be a pyramid.

Inside the prisons, everyone felt they were dying; they were thirsty and hungry but couldn't leave because they were tormented by demons of fear and guilt. There were pyramids from all religions and unfortunately also from Christianity.

Then the prophet showed me something that filled me with great pain. We were facing the pyramids filled with Christians - children of God -, and in the hands of every man at the summit was an oil lamp, many of which were out.

They spoke about Jesus; men and women called by God and anointed by God, but they had allowed their own names to grow more important in their own lives than Jesus'. People inside the prisons clamored the names of these men and women and relayed on them to ease their pains.

I wept because I saw us, millions of Christians there; either one way or another, we had been made captive to *Babylon*'s system. I also saw myself; I was on a throne judging others and covered by the filthiness of my own righteousness.

When I saw myself, I fell prostrate before Jesus in deep repentance. I then saw a vision within a vision, and I was taken to another place for a moment. Jesus wanted to show me what would give me the standard by which to never again judge others and to begin my own exit out of *Babylon*.

I found myself facing a gigantic mouth like that of a whale. From inside it a force would come out and suction me to the inside while I was crying out the name of Jesus. Suddenly, the force stopped and I heard the voice of the Lord speaking like thunder: **"Tell me, what is more powerful than death and fear?"**

" I don't know Lord, I don't know" I answered Him trembling.

Then He told me, **"It's temptation!"** He then added, **"if you are still standing, it's because of my grace. I know the heart of every man, and if I caused you to face what you could not overcome, you would fall like the rest of them. All men can fall into the same abomination; no one is better than the next. If they have not fallen, it is because of My grace and My love that sustain them."**

I clearly understood how all of us can err and fall. Even having the best of intentions, we can fall victims of *Babylon*. I began a process in which I asked God to show me how much of *Babylon* was in me, and how to exit that system, which kills the life of God within us.

I returned from that vision to the city where the prophet was waiting for me. At that moment I heard the voice of the Father pleading, "The doors of *Babylon* are open to allow all of those who hear My voice to leave. I am calling out from My holy mountain, Come out from there, MY PEOPLE! Only those who humble themselves can exit. Only those who love My name more than theirs can see the way out. Many of them touched my heart deeply as they cried for their cities and their nations. I have next to me a flask filled with their tears, and each one is a treasure to Me.

127

But when I raised them up and gave them a name, they extolled themselves and formed a kingdom for themselves. They laid down laws I did not give them, and they confiscated my flock. They were imprisoned by *Babylon* who gave them a name to be recognized among the nations. Their lamps have not been extinguished by reason of My love, but not much time is left."

As the Father spoke, I remembered something I had heard inside His heart, in that place like the Holy of Holies where all the wounds against love are. His heart overflowed with intense pain coming from a sore that bled incessantly. My body cramped just by looking at it. I heard the voice of the Holy Spirit telling me, "My people have gotten so accustomed to saying, 'I am from such and such church, or from Apostle so and so, or from the such and such network, or from this denomination or that,' which seems like something normal, permissible and even blessed by Me, when this is an abomination that hurts Me deeply." The Father then said: **"I will not put up with this anymore."**

I wept a lot because I am guilty of those wounds. However, ever since that day I decided to dedicate my life to love and to do whatever is required so that God sees His Church united by the bonds of the Spirit and free from the system that separates and destroys us.

The theme of *Babylon* is a book in itself. It is the whole structure of the kingdom of darkness, making it impossible for me to break it down in one single chapter.

3. WHO IS *BABYLON?*

The visions speak for themselves. *Babylon* is the religious system that kills the spiritual life of the Church and renders us inept to reign. *Babylon* has existed ever since religious systems existed, no matter what these may be. This is the spirit that took over the Jewish priesthood during the time of Jesus. *Babylon* is not the Roman Catholic Church as some think; it is a whole system that has the form of godliness yet lacks the life of God. The "form" will always resist the *"Life"* and end up destroying the vessel. It is a hypocritical system that says one thing and lives another.

Jesus speaks in an imperative manner to HIS PEOPLE to exit *Babylon:*

And I heard another voice from heaven saying, "Come out of her, my people, lest you share in her sins, and lest you receive of her plagues."   Revelation 18:4

He is not speaking to a pagan people - He is talking to His Church. We all come from *Babylon;* nobody escapes. Those of us who came out of the Roman Church were impregnated with religion. We exchange idolatry for the richness of the Bible but continue calling "church" and even "temple" the rock - and - cement buildings where we gather. We continue using phrases such as, *"See you in church on Sunday,"* When we – the people - are the temple of God.

We embraced the reformation principles Martin Luther left us without realizing he also came from the Roman *Babylonian* system. He gave us the essence of the message of salvation we now have,

129

but brought with it the same system of having church exclusively within the four walls of a building which little by little does away with the life of the true Church.

Babylon makes us follow man under the guise of following God. We continue viewing the leadership as the anointed ones who are closer to God than the rest of the people. We continue separating the priests from the laymen. People depend more on the hand of man than that of God. They make the man or woman of God the source of their answers. As leaders, we do not propel people to depend on God and to know Him, because, in a certain way, we like them to depend on us. And unintentionally, whereas our words speak of loving God and following Him, our religious system makes us continue perpetuating their depending on us. If we are Heaven's ambassadors, we need to speak and to see ourselves as manifesting Heaven, not just reproducing men's systems.

When God revealed Himself to me, He showed me how much *Babylon* was in me. He allowed me to see how much I enjoyed man's reverence and being the great woman of God for my nation even though it was done unconsciously. He made me understand how each one of us has collaborated in dividing the Body of Christ and how this is nothing but the *Babylonian* system in which we operate. When I understood this, I called out to His name to get me out of *Babylon* and help me get others out.

My message is not to get people out of churches but to get the churches out of *Babylon* – the Pastor and the people - and bring them into the Kingdom og God. People come to Jesus, but they never destroy the *Babylonian* structure from whence they have come throughout their generations. It's easier to attend a worship service on Sunday than to take authority and become the kings and priests He wants us to be. This system only has space for a few people to grow and change, but the Kingdom of God is not like it, everyone can become what God designed for them to be.

4. THE EFFECTS OF BABYLON ON TODAY'S CHURCH

a) *Babylon* is confusion which always twists God's message. Its main intent is to separate Heaven from Earth, which will deny and obstruct the Heavenly reality inside the believer. Jesus came to join Heaven and Earth and to give us the fullness of His life so we could truly be His Body on Earth. The religious structures upon which we place divine revelation must be destroyed if we want to have the authority to reign.

b) *Babylon calls itself Queen, Mistress of the Kingdoms.* She wants to have the kingdom so Jesus doesn't have it. This causes people to not recognize Christ in His Kingdom. They receive Him as their savior, but not as the sovereign Lord over their lives. It enables them to see Christ filled with His glory in Heaven above, yet not the Christ living in their hearts who capable of healing all their sicknesses and solve all their problems. *Babylon* "has to have control" over everything and will never release it to the Holy Spirit.

The Church, deceived by *Babylon*, moans for God to descend His glory upon her. They fast and pray, waiting for Him to one day send the revolving fire of His glory that will usher in the awaited revival.

Beloved of my Father, do we not realize that it's Jesus in all His glory who inhabits us? What different, more powerful glory can come than the one Jesus has already granted us?

"And the glory that You gave Me I have given them, that they may be one just as We are one."   John 17:22

Do you realize how this spirit comes to confound and rob us from the glory Jesus already gave us?

In the **Book of Revelation,** Jesus reveals Himself to John in His glory so that by contrast we can identify *Babylon* and come out of it. I am not saying that we need to leave our congregations; I am saying that whole congregations need to come out of *Babylon* and become re-structured to God's model: a Church united by the Holy Spirit, blessing and spiritually governing over the cities.

It's in that glory that Jesus gives the message to the seven churches, our manual on how to enter the most powerful authority to govern with Jesus.

This message is not addressed to the observance of the commandments of the Old Covenant; instead, it denounces the religious *Babylonian* spirit and the manner it operates. It stealthily creeps up in the life of the believers, robbing them of the life and the fire of their first love, until it leaves them without any authority or power.

THE SEVEN LETTERS TO THE CHURCHES: THE KEYS TO OUR GOVERNMENT

Although this is not one of the main themes that reveal the interpretation of the *Book of Revelation,* I include it here as the *Victory over Babylon.* Each letter is a key that will allow us to defeat the *spirit of religion,* and destroy *Babylon,* the *sixth theme of interpretation.*

Jesus manifests His own characteristics in each letter, which helps us obtain the prize that will allow us to govern. These are doors of infinite revelation to reign in the here and now.

1. EPHESUS

"To the angel of the church of Ephesus write, 'These things says He who holds the seven stars in His right hand, who walks in the midst of the seven golden lampstands: I know your works, your labor, your patience, and that you cannot bear those who are evil. And you have tested those who say they are apostles and are not, and have

133

found them liars; and you have persevered and have patience, and have labored for My name's sake and have not become weary.

Nevertheless I have this against you, that you have left your first love.

Remember therefore from where you have fallen; repent and do the first works, or else I will come to you quickly and remove your lampstand from its place—unless you repent. But this you have, that you hate the deeds of the Nicolaitans, which I also hate.

He who has an ear, let him hear what the Spirit says to the churches. To him who overcomes I will give to eat from the Tree of Life, which is in the midst of the Paradise of God."   *Revelation 2:1-7*

Ephesus: Its name means "desirable." The theme of this letter is: **true love is what crowns us.** Jesus introduces Himself to us as the One who is amidst the candlesticks. Jesus is the One who is in control of the Church; man is not. Pure love is what positions us in the center of *Paradise,* which is the place of ruling. Love is the *fountain of life* that feeds the nations and opposes *Nicolaitanism,* the hierarchical religious system that raises leadership atop a pedestal and takes the power and authority away from lay people, who are also children of God. *Nicolaitanism* raises its own kingdom and does not let God build His up. It steers the believers to depend on men who are at the head, not on THE head who is Jesus. Although an order of authority exists in the Church, our spiritual dependence must be on Jesus.

Christ is the *Tree of Life;* this represents the life of the Spirit as opposed to the *Tree of Good and Evil,* which is based on human reasoning. The first one raises a system of life, whereas the second, one of death. Love and our marriage commitment to Christ lead us to the dominion of all things.

2. SMYRNA

"And to the angel of the church in Smyrna write, 'These things says the First and the Last, who was dead, and came to life:
I know your works, tribulation, and poverty (but you are rich); and I know the blasphemy of those who say they are Jews and are not, but are a synagogue of Satan. Do not fear any of those things which you are about to suffer. Indeed, the devil is about to throw some of you into prison, that you may be tested, and you will have tribulation ten days. Be faithful until death, and I will give you the crown of life.
He who has an ear, let him hear what the Spirit says to the churches. He who overcomes shall not be hurt by the second death." Revelation 2:8-11 NKJV

Smyrna: Its name means "martyr" or "fragrance." Its theme is: **The keys against death.** Jesus introduces Himself as the First and the Last, the One who is alive but was dead. Jesus was the One who defeated death, the beginning and the end of all things. This is the key to vanquish death and to inherit the *Crown of Life.* We have to remain faithful unto death for this one: die to this world to live in Jesus. When we are able to see death as a victory and when we are clothed with our heavenly house, death cannot intimidate us. It's in this victory that we obtain the authority to resurrect the dead and transform dead territories so they can live. Having death under our feet enables us to defeat the devil in all his ways.

And they overcame him by the blood of the Lamb and by the word of their testimony, and they loved not their lives unto the death.   Revelation 12:11

I am crucified with Christ, nevertheless I live; yet not I, but Christ liveth in me. And the life which I now live in the flesh, I live by the faith of the Son of God, who loved me and gave Himself for me.   Galatians 2:20

This key gives us the ability to understand how tribulations are instruments that position us more and more into greater, higher - authority ranks.

To vanquish death in all its forms - fear, sicknesses, bitterness, and sin - enables us live in the spheres of what is Eternal.

This key changes our perspective to see things from their temporary state to see them in their eternal function and purpose.

3. PERGAMOS

"And to the angel of the church in Pergamos write, 'These things says He who has the sharp two-edged sword: I know your works, and where you dwell, where Satan's throne is. And you hold fast to My name, and did not deny My faith even in the days in which Antipas was My faithful martyr, who was killed among you, where Satan dwells. But I have a few things against you, because you have there those who hold the doctrine of Balaam, who

taught Balak to put a stumbling block before the children of Israel, to eat things sacrificed to idols, and to commit sexual immorality. Thus you also have those who hold the doctrine of the Nicolaitans, which thing I hate. Repent, or else I will come to you quickly and will fight against them with the sword of My mouth.

"He who has an ear, let him hear what the Spirit says to the churches. To him who overcomes I will give some of the hidden manna to eat. And I will give him a white stone, and on the stone a new name written which no one knows except him who receives it."

Revelation 2:12 -17

Pergamos: Its name means "high place" and its theme is **the power of the Word.** Jesus introduces Himself as the One who has the two-edged sword and who releases judgment with the authority of His Word. Those who govern with Him must have authority to judge and see all things from God's righteous heart. We have to tower above the obscure levels of our own opinion to judge with righteous judgment.

This is the key to conquer every circumstance even if it's satan's throne on Earth. It's the key to overcome the power of greed, money and the desire to be in good standing with men rather than God.

Balaam, the prophet in Numbers 22-24 was mentioned in this letter. He sold his message and his call for money, as nowadays there are those who do so, too, today. To eat things sacrificed to idols and commit fornication speaks to us about how the Word of God is spoken with indolence and lukewarmth. This attitude

137

is contrary to the sharp two-edged sword that confronts and discerns the soul and the spirit, thereby converting the heart.

The prize is the *hidden manna,* the true revelation necessary to rule. It is the provision of Heaven that comes over the givers, those who divest themselves of their wealth for the love of God's work and their fellow men, defeating *Mammon,* the god of riches.

God gives us a new name here; our authority and our identity are in that name. Through this new name we can subdue nations, loose the loins of kings, straighten crooked places, open iron gates, and receive from God His treasures.

> *Thus saith the LORD to His anointed, to Cyrus, whose right hand I have held to* **subdue nations before him;** *and I will* **loose the loins of kings** *to open before him the two leaved gates; and the gates shall not be shut: I will go before thee, and make the crooked places straight; I will break in pieces the gates of brass, and cut in sunder the bars of iron. And I will give thee* **the treasures of darkness** *and* **hidden riches of secret places,** *that thou mayest know that I, the LORD,* **who call thee by thy name,** *am the God of Israel.* Isaiah 45:1-3

4. THYATIRA

> *"And to the angel of the church in Thyatira write, 'These things says the Son of God, who has eyes like a flame of fire, and His feet like fine brass:*
> *"I know your works, love, service, faith, and your patience; and as for your works, the last are more than the first.*

138

Nevertheless I have a few things against you, because you allow that woman Jezebel, who calls herself a prophetess, to teach and seduce My servants to commit sexual immorality and eat things sacrificed to idols. And I gave her time to repent of her sexual immorality, and she did not repent.

Indeed I will cast her into a sickbed, and those who commit adultery with her into great tribulation, unless they repent of their deeds.

I will kill her children with death, and all the churches shall know that I am He who searches the minds and hearts. And I will give to each one of you according to your works.

Now to you I say, and to the rest in Thyatira, as many as do not have this doctrine, who have not known the depths of Satan, as they say, I will put on you no other burden. But hold fast what you have till I come.

And he who overcomes, and keeps My works until the end, to him I will give power over the nations—

He shall rule them with a rod of iron;

They shall be dashed to pieces like the potter's vessels'—as I also have received from My Father; and I will give him the morning star.

"He who has an ear, let him hear what the Spirit says to the churches."   Revelation 2:18-29 NKJV

Thyatira: Its name is uncertain; its true meaning is unknown. Its theme is: **the key that discerns what comes from God and what comes from man.** Jesus introduces Himself as the One Who has eyes like fire and feet like fine brass.

This key is the one that determines the authority to rule nations. To govern is to judge and execute righteousness, but it has to be according to the *eyes of God*. He sees each one of our actions from different angles. We see the facts in black and white; this is the Tree of Good and Evil. The eyes of God analyze every circumstance that surrounds each case, the extenuating and the aggravating.

... and shall make Him of quick understanding in the fear of the LORD; and He shall not judge after the sight of His eyes, neither reprove after the hearing of His ears. But with righteousness shall He judge the poor, and reprove with equity for the meek of the earth; and He shall smite the earth with the rod of His mouth, and with the breath of His lips shall He slay the wicked.   *Isaiah 11:3-4*

Jezebel is the authority-usurping spirit who seeks her own kingdom above God's, judges through the limited and inquisition-like eyes of religion, and who governs through principles of fear, intimidation and control over people. She does not allow them to depend on God, but forces them to depend on man, making God's children spiritually crippled. Her messages are attractive for the soul, but lack commitment to God.

Jezebel leads to spiritual fornication, which is to please oneself with the warmth of a relationship without the commitment of a marriage; it is to try to achieve moments of intimacy with the Holy Spirit without a real determination and covenant to follow Jesus wherever He goes. We see this clearly explained in Chapter 14 of the *Book of Revelation* where the 144,000 chosen are described and how they do not spiritually defile themselves and achieve it through their total commitment to Jesus.

These are the ones who were not defiled with women,
(Jezebel) for they are virgins (Consecrated). These are
the ones who follow the Lamb wherever He goes. These
were redeemed from among men, being the firstfruits to
God and to the Lamb.

Revelation 14:4
(parenthesis by autor)

Jezebel is not only a spirit but also a doctrine where the eyes of men are diverted and focused on man rather than on God. *To know the depths of satan* has to do with entering into intimacy with him, making pacts with his tricks and seductions. We must gain the understanding of the strategies and works of the devil without getting involved with him.

Fear of man and his dominion over others is the essence of a religious system, which shrewdly disguises itself as "godliness" and is difficult to identify. This is why Jesus manifests Himself with *eyes of fire* so through Him we can see its fraudulent works of darkness, cloaked in their false light.

... having a form of godliness but denying the power
thereof. From such turn away.   *2 Timothy 3:5*

Religiosity is the toughest mountain hindering us from governing with Christ. Jesus broke the religious system of His time with an iron rod. To the person who overcomes this, Jesus gives His authority over the nations. He also manifests Himself in this letter as the *bright morning star* in our lives.

We have also a more sure word of prophecy, unto which

141

*ye do well that ye take heed, as unto a light that shineth in a dark place, until the day dawn and the **day star arises in your hearts.*** 2 Peter 1:19

This is the shining glow that becomes visible in every believer when, as the vessel that contains Christ incarnated, he has conformed to His Word. The vessel and the Word are - and walk - in agreement.

If the seven churches form the candlestick of the light of God, Thyatira would be at the center as a vital government message.

5. SARDIS

"And to the angel of the church in Sardis write, These things says He who has the seven Spirits of God and the seven stars:

'I know your works, that you have a name that you are alive, but you are dead.

Be watchful, and strengthen the things which remain, that are ready to die, for I have not found your works perfect before God.

Remember therefore how you have received and heard; hold fast and repent. Therefore if you will not watch, I will come upon you as a thief, and you will not know what hour I will come upon you.

You have a few names even in Sardis who have not defiled their garments; and they shall walk with Me in white, for they are worthy.

He who overcomes shall be clothed in white garments, and I will not blot out his name from the Book of Life; but

I will confess his name before My Father and before His angels.
"He who has an ear, let him hear what the Spirit says to the churches." ' Revelation 3:1-6

Sardis: Its name means "Prince of Joy." Its theme is, **the key to know the multiple manifestations of the Spirit and of the angels that are granted to us.** Jesus introduces Himself as the One who has the seven Spirits of God and the seven stars.

A person whose life is not immersed in Him will eventually die, possessing the name of one who lives but is indeed dead. This key requires a holiness that can only be obtained by knowing God every day and fusing evermore with Him. His seven Spirits are the ones who reveal Him and give life to the Church. Our growth with Him depends on our knowing Him in each one of these seven characteristics.

*And the Spirit of the LORD shall rest upon Him, **the Spirit of wisdom and understanding, the Spirit of counsel and might, the Spirit of knowledge and of the fear of the LORD.** "* Isaiah 11:2

In the following passage in Isaiah we see how the manifestations of the seven Spirits are key to govern with righteous judgments. However, these, in turn, broaden, as we understand their functions.

The Spirit of the Lord GOD *is upon Me, because the LORD hath anointed **Me to preach** good tidings unto the meek. He hath sent me to **bind up the brokenhearted,** to proclaim liberty to the captives, and the opening*

143

of the prison to them that are bound, To proclaim the **acceptable year of the LORD,** *and the day of vengeance of our God; to* **comfort** *all that mourn, To appoint unto them that mourn in Zion, to give unto them beauty for ashes, the oil of* **joy for mourning,** *the garment of praise for the spirit of heaviness, that they might be called trees of righteousness, the planting of the LORD, that He might be glorified. And they shall* **build the wastes of old,** *they shall raise up the former desolations, and they shall* **repair the waste cities,** *the desolations of many generations.*

Isaiah 61:1-4

To govern with Christ refers to all those things that lead to the restoration and re-building of that which was lost.

Jesus rules with His angels and has granted them to co-labor alongside us. All throughout the *Book of Revelation* we see the angels interacting with the believers and with John to the point that the apostle calls them "fellow servants."

It's through our contact with the Holy Spirit and the fear of God that we remain in holiness, robed in white raiment and endure in the life of God.

It's in this key that God grants us, apart from being robed in white raiment and our names inscribed in the Book of Life, that our names will be confessed before the Father and His angels.

There is major authority here. When our names resonate inside the Father, angels rush to our aid. The angels know those who are sealed by the Father.

... For He shall give His angels charge over thee to keep thee in all thy ways, they shall bear thee up in their hands, lest thou dash thy foot against a stone. Thou shalt tread upon the lion and adder; the young lion and the dragon shalt thou trample underfoot...Because he hath set his love upon Me, therefore will I deliver him; I will set him on high, because he hath known My name.

Psalm 91:11-14

6. PHILADELPHIA

"And to the angel of the church in Philadelphia write, These things says He who is holy, He who is true, 'He who has the key of David, He who opens and no one shuts, and shuts and no one opens:

"I know your works. See, I have set before you an open door, and no one can shut it; for you have a little strength, have kept My word, and have not denied My name. Indeed I will make those of the synagogue of Satan, who say they are Jews and are not, but lie—indeed I will make them come and worship before your feet, and to know that I have loved you.

Because you have kept My command to persevere, I also will keep you from the hour of trial which shall come upon the whole world, to test those who dwell on the earth. Behold, I am coming quickly! Hold fast what you have, that no one may take your crown.

He who overcomes, I will make him a pillar in the temple of My God, and he shall go out no more. I will write on him the name of My God and the name of the city of My God, the New Jerusalem, which comes down out of heaven

145

from My God. And I will write on him My new name.
He who has an ear, let him hear what the Spirit says to
the churches. "   *Revelation. 3:7-13*

Philadelphia: Its name means "fraternal love," and its theme
is: **the key of David.** Jesus introduces Himself as holy and true,
having the keys of David that open doors but no one shuts and
shuts, but no one opens.

Indeed all who delight in piety and are determined to
live a devoted and godly life in Christ Jesus will meet
with persecution [will be made to suffer because of their
religious stand].   *2 Timothy 3:12 AMP*

... if we suffer, we shall also reign with Him...
                    2 Timothy 2:12

The Kingdom is given to us through our overcoming tribulation
and persecution. The devil wants to shut all doors on us, but the
One who has the keys to open and shut is Jesus, not satan.

Once more, the keys of the Kingdom are handed over to us
through Christ revealing Himself in our lives, which causes the
gates of Hades not to prevail against the Kingdom children.

Jesus reveals Himself here as holy and truthful. To live
conformed to His holiness and truth is what will always keep
the doors open for us to do the work of God and to establish His
Kingdom.

Truth is immovable; all that is false and illusory inevitably ends up shattered at the feet of truth. Remaining in truth makes all systems around us begin to topple. Because lies and falsehood cannot stand truth, they will persecute it unto death as they did with Jesus, but in the end, truth resurrects and triumphs.

One day I had a vision and saw Moses standing in front of the Red Sea. His rod represented the Word of truth that Jehovah had given him: **"He shall deliver His people."** Moses stood holding his rod up high until everything began to shake; the winds became stronger, and the waters could no longer remain in their place and had to open up. Then I heard the Lord say, Heaven and Earth shall pass away but the Word of the Lord remains forever.

To stand on the truth at whatever the cost shall always open doors, part the seas, form pathways in rugged places, split mountains, shut lions' mouths, and shatter Hell's gates. This is one of the Most High's great keys of government.

Truth and holiness are God's fortified castle, the walls and the columns that support it.

Columns are a symbol of the foundation of what has been established to support a building. They imply strength, rectitude, and composure. In the natural, this is what keeps the house stable and the most secure place in an earthquake.

And he raised up the pillars before the temple, one on the right hand and the other on the left, and called the name of that one on the right hand Jachin [that is, He shall establish], and the name of that on the left Boaz [that is, In it is strength].　　　*2 Chronicles 3:17 AMP*

147

To live and express His holiness and truth is not mimicking them but allowing Him to produce them in us. When He encounters vessels where He is free to manifest Who He is, He will place in them His greatest prize; they will carry the name of God on their foreheads and will genuinely be the heavenly city walking on Earth.

7. LAODICEA

"And to the angel of the church of the Laodiceans write, 'These things says the Amen, the Faithful and True Witness, the Beginning of the creation of God:
I know your works, that you are neither cold nor hot. I could wish you were cold or hot.
So then, because you are lukewarm, and neither cold nor hot, I will vomit you out of My mouth.
Because you say, 'I am rich, have become wealthy, and have need of nothing'—and do not know that you are wretched, miserable, poor, blind, and naked—
I counsel you to buy from Me gold refined in the fire, that you may be rich; and white garments, that you may be clothed, that the shame of your nakedness may not be revealed; and anoint your eyes with eye salve, that you may see.
As many as I love, I rebuke and chasten. Therefore be zealous and repent.
Behold, I stand at the door and knock. If anyone hears My voice and opens the door, I will come in to him and dine with him, and he with Me.
To him who overcomes I will grant to sit with Me on My throne, as I also overcame and sat down with My Father

on His throne.
"He who has an ear, let him hear what the Spirit says to
the churches." Revelation 3:14-22

Laodicea: It´s name means "lukewarm" and its theme is **sit at God's throne with Jesus.** Jesus introduces Himself as the Amen, the True and Faithful Witness, the Beginning of the Creation.

The challenge here is to defeat religion at one of its most important disguises, its external appearances, to say one thing and live a different reality - blinded and thinking we possess it all because of superficial success. Jesus manifests Himself as the Amen and trains us not to be double-faced but to live the certainty of everything He is.

The government key here is to become an experiential witness of Heaven. To see and hear what the Kingdom of God says and does is pivotal to reigning in the spiritual spheres.

Jesus manifests Himself as the *Beginning of all Creation* because all things were created precisely from the realm of the Spirit. To penetrate His invisible Kingdom, to hear and see Jesus and the Father is what truly makes us witnesses.

As we previously saw, the Spirit of Prophecy is the testimony of Jesus. It's through understanding and continually entering the Spirit that we will receive the salve to see as God sees. Our fellowship with God and our longing to become clothed with Jesus will form in us our true raiment, which is our heavenly house.

To see ourselves as He sees us is the mirror that confronts us to die to all that is worldly, and in this manner His fire purifies us as gold.

The Lord's Supper is the greatest inheritance He left us, through it we are transformed into His image to sit with Him in His throne and reign with Him in the here and the now.[15]

This letter is not a call to salvation but to reign; to allow Him to take the throne and government of our lives to make us kings and priests unto God the Father.

---

[15] My book *Eat of my flesh and Drink of my Blood*, shares in depth on the riches of the Lord's Supper.

12 THE MANIFESTATION OF JESUS

1. A SPIRITUAL KINGDOM

I n chapter 7 we spoke about the *power* and the *purpose* of our Messiah's *First Coming*. Now we are going to understand further how His marvelous Kingdom manifests on Earth. This is the *seventh theme of interpratation.*

During Jesus' time, the people of Israel expected the Messiah to sit on *Jerusalem's* political throne. When He didn't, and thereby established that His Kingdom was not of this world, many of the Jews who followed Him ended up disappointed, among whom were Judas Iscariot, the Zealots, and most of the members of the Sanhedrin. This caused them to eliminate Jesus as the possible Messiah and continued waiting for the One who would fulfill this expectation. This idea still prevails and spurs the thinking of many to believe the Kingdom has not come. They yearned for a physical kingdom therefore they rejected the idea of an invisible one.

Jesus clearly told them how His Kingdom on Earth was to be:

*Jesus answered, "My kingdom is **not of this world.** If My* *kingdom were of this world, My servants would fight, so that I should not be delivered to the Jews; but now My kingdom is not from here."*   *John 18:36*

*Asked by the Pharisees when the Kingdom of God would come, He replied to them by saying, "The kingdom of God does not come with signs to be observed or with visible display, Nor will people say, Look! Here [it is]! or, See, [it is] there! For behold, the kingdom of God is within you [in your hearts] and **among you [surrounding you].**"*
Luke 17:20-21 AMP

Even though the Kingdom of God is invisible, it has to impact the Earth through the sons of God, and, by the mighty hand of the Lord the results will be visible. Righteousness is going to be established, evil will be judged, and the knowledge of God's manifested glory will cover the Earth as the waters cover the sea.

So let us carefully analyze this topic:

Jesus came to bring His Father's Kingdom and He did not fail in His mission. He is seated at the Father's right hand, crowned as King of kings and Lord of lords governing together with His Church, which is His spouse. She is flesh of His flesh and bone of His bones and legitimately His Body.

The Church has the authority from her head who is Christ, and has the victory over everything Jesus paid for her at the cross of Calvary. She is the heavenly city in the middle of which Jesus is providing all her needs.

From the beginning to the end of the Old Testament, Jesus, being the Spirit of Prophecy, announced His coming in the flesh and the establishment of His Kingdom. He does not separate one from the other. The coming of Messiah is the hub of God's message and our inheritance. To understand in depth the work of Messiah, we have to realize that He operates simultaneously in two dimensions, Heaven and Earth, which are united in Jesus, if He reigns in Heaven, He does so on Earth, too.

If then you were raised with Christ, seek those things which are above, where Christ is, sitting at the right hand of God. **Set your mind on things above, not on things on the earth.** Colossians 3:1-2

2. PATMOS, FOURTH VISION

Once again I found myself on the mountain from where milk and honey flow and from which new wine with an exquisite fragrance sprung forth. I was delighting myself, facing the clear water fountain filled with lights that descended, forming a great river that flooded the valley. I then saw many other mountains flowing out from the great mountain; waters of life, honey, and new wine flowed forth from each one and filled the Heaven as far as my eye could see.[16]

Altogether with the great mountain, they conformed to Jesus and came from Him as I had seen the first time; but this time, a new dimension opened underneath my feet.

From behind the great mountain, an intense light stronger

---

[16] Scriptures that confirm this vision: Joel 3:18 and Zechariah 13:1

than the sun's appeared and in the center of this light was One resembling the Son of God seated on His throne. It was made of fire but different from the one on Earth; it blazed but did not burn, and it was as transparent and translucent like millions of lit sparkles. From its center a river of fire descended all the way to Earth.

Then the great mountain descended and filled the whole Earth. A great joy came to Heaven, and a majestic symphony overflowed it. A myriad of angels sang, "Hallelujah, Hallelujah our God Almighty reigns!" I then saw how on the hillsides of the mountain there was formed what appeared to be a gold overlay that covered all the nations, and I heard the voice of the Holy Spirit say, "Herein, the Tabernacle of God with men."

I saw how the river of fire that came from the throne of Jesus was poured over the heads of many people and the converted into mountains. I then heard a voice come out from the fire, and when they heard it, the mountains grew taller and stronger.

The river of fire is never quenched because it was established for eternity.

Mount Sion- The Seat of His Goverment

From the place I was standing, I was able to understand everything with great clarity and knew that I was watching the day the Holy Spirit was poured over all flesh. The holy mountain of God was established on that day and the devil's government was fully defeated. From that moment on, the only one who holds the keys to rule over death and Hell, is Jesus Christ.

The passage of Daniel where he sees the rock coming out of Heaven, which destroys the image that symbolizes the *Babylonian* system[17] came to mind:

*Then the iron, the clay, the bronze, the silver, and the gold were crushed together, and became like chaff from the summer threshing floors; the wind carried them away so that no trace of them was found. And the stone that struck the image became **a great mountain and filled the whole earth.*** Daniel 2:35

*The mount of Zion is over the Earth and it is the government of God that was established once and for all. But you have come to **Mount Zion** and to the city of the living God, the heavenly Jerusalem, to an innumerable company of angels...* Hebrews 12:22

His Kingdom is invisible and in the midst of us. The issue for us is that the Church has not known how to enter and live in it because they have grown poorly in the realm of the Spirit. Besides, the placing of His Kingdom as a "future" manifestation removes from the Church the possibility to enter into it **now.**

It's an indisputable reality for everyone that Jesus is in the midst of us as King of kings and Lord of lords and if we understand what this means in its fullness, we will see the Church enter into its highest glory manifestation. There is a clear manifestation in the Bible of His coming in the spiritual

---

[17] The whole Babylonian system represented by this one statue is conformed by four empires, Babylon, Persia, Greece, and Rome. They are all one demonic structure manifested in four different ways that ruled the known world throughout different eras.

sense, which we can lay a hold of and which does not contradict the fact that one day He will manifest Himself again in a visible and tangible form in a glorified body.

What we have to understand is that when Jesus said the He would come again to be with us, He didn't always refer to His *Second Coming* in the flesh; most of time He was talking about His spiritual presence among His Church.

In Section IV, Instrument 1, of this book I will lay out the Greek words that demostrate the different ways He comes to us or will come in His *Second Coming.*

During His physical presence on Earth, He could not live in the hearts of believers. He never called His disciples to receive Him in their hearts, because that couldn't happen until the day of Pentecost. This is why He said in John 16:7 and John 14:23 that He had to leave and would come again with His Father to make His dwelling place in us.

*Nevertheless I tell you the truth. **It is to your advantage that I go away;** for if I do not go away, the Helper will not come to you; **but if I depart, I will send Him to you.*** John 16:7

In My Father's house are many mansions; if it were not so, I would have told you. I go to prepare a place for you. And if I go and prepare a place for you, I will come again and receive you to Myself; that where I am, there you may be also. John 14:2-3

I will not leave you orphans; I will come to you.
"A little while longer and the world will see Me no more,
but you will see Me. Because I live, you will live also.
At that day you will know that I am in My Father, and you
in Me, and I in you.   *John 14:18-20*

Jesus answered and said to him, "If anyone loves Me, he
will keep My word; and My Father will love him, and We
will come to him and make Our home with him.
                                                          John 14:23

In most of the Scriptures where His Second Coming is mentioned four Greek words are used to describe different manifestations of this happening: **Parousia, Epifania, Apocalipsis and Erchomai;** These refer to His presence in the Church as the temple of God or to a manifestation of His glory that judges evil. (See Instrument 1 in Section IV)

Most of these scriptures referred to the end of the old system and were fulfilled during the fall of *Jerusalem* and the destruction of the temple in the year 70 A.D. Others could refer to Jesus coming at the end of all the eras to execute His final judgment.

Teaching them to observe all things whatsoever I have
commanded you: and, lo, I am with you always, even
unto the end of the world. Amen.   *Mathew 28:20*

And while they looked steadfastly toward heaven as He
went up, behold, two men stood by them in white apparel,
who also said, "Men of Galilee, why do you stand gazing
up into heaven? This same Jesus, who was taken up from

*you into heaven, will so come in like manner as you saw
Him go into heaven."*   *Acts 1:10-11*

3. THE PURPOSE OF MESSIAH'S KINGDOM

The Kingdom's purpose is at the center of God's heart, and this
is what fills the Earth with the KNOWLEDGE of the glory of God
as the waters cover the sea.

He will do this through a people who know Him and manifest
Him en every sphere of society. People who understand them are
kings and priests with this mission among the nations.

We have to establish the mountain of God above *every* mountain
of influence on Earth: politics, economy, health, arts, media,
movies, energy resources, space science, fashion, etc.

The Kingdom culture has to conquer every culture on Earth.
We, the children of God, are not part of Earth's culture, nor is our
citizenship of this world. We no longer belong here; we belong to
Heaven.

To understand these things changes our way of thinking, and
instead of waiting for when we escape here to avoid the destroction
of the whole world, we begin to think about how to pray to win
our nations so none is lost.

God wants to make us overcomers and make us shine, thereby
shaming the strong and the wise of this world. He wants to
demonstrate to the devil that His children are capable, through
their humanity redeemed by Jesus, of destroying all his structures
and plans of destruction.

1. THE CLOUDS IN THE KINGDOM OF GOD

T he majority of the theological currents, although not all of them, have always believed that Jesus will literally return in the midst of clouds. But what would happen if Scripture itself shows us that the clouds Jesus was referring to are not those puffy vapor masses that float in the sky?

Our understanding opens up when we see the intimate relationship existing between the abode of God and the clouds. This is the *eighth basic theme of interpretation.*

Dost thou know the (difference) balancings of the clouds, the wondrous works of Him who is perfect in knowledge?
Job 37:16

Not only that, but can anyone understand the spreadings of the clouds or the thundering noise of His tabernacle?
Job 36:29

He made darkness His secret place; His tabernacle round

about Him was dark waters and thick clouds of the skies.
Psalm 18:11

Clouds and darkness are round about Him; righteousness
and judgment are the habitation of His throne.
Psalm 97:2

... who layeth the beams of His chambers in the waters,
who maketh the clouds His chariot, who walketh upon the
wings of the wind;... *Psalm 104:3*

God's manifestation in the clouds is not a single event as traditional theologies suggest: *He lives surrounded by them.*

Now that we have gained understanding about this, we're going to explore the deeper meaning of what Messiah wanted to make known to us.

Jesus clearly announced how He would come to dwell in the Spirit in the midst of His Church.

When the Son of Man shall come in His glory and all the
holy angels with Him, **then shall He sit upon the throne**
of His glory,*...* *Matthew 25:31*

We see here that **His coming in the clouds is directly related to His sitting on the throne** and not with a physical coming. This is clear to us now that we have been studying the *key themes* of interpretation.

This is of **vital importance** because, if Jesus is not yet seated on

160

the throne at the right hand of the Father, then He is not King of kings either.

Jesus has already been crowned, and this title has already been given to Him.

He declares to the high priest when this would happen:

*Jesus said unto him, "Thou hast said; nevertheless I say unto you, **hereafter shall ye see** the Son of Man sitting at the right hand of Power, and coming in the clouds of heaven".*
*Then the high priest rent his clothes, saying, "He hath spoken blasphemy! What further need have we of witnesses? Behold, now ye have **heard his blasphemy!"***
Matthew 26:64-65

He told him, **"Hereafter** shall you see the Son of Man sitting at the right hand of the Power of God and coming in the clouds of heaven." He did not mean in 2000 years. *Hereafter* means from now on.

For the religious mind, that was considered blasphemy; and for many whose preconceived ideas do not allow them to see this truth, they, too, will consider it blasphemy.

The prophet Daniel had a clear vision of the moment when Jesus was to take up the throne.

*I saw in the night visions, and behold, **one like the Son of Man came with the clouds of heaven,** and came to*

161

the Ancient of Days, and they brought Him near before Him. And there was given Him dominion and glory and a Kingdom, that all people, nations, and languages should serve Him. His dominion is an everlasting dominion, which shall not pass away, and His Kingdom that which shall not be destroyed.

*... until the Ancient of Days came, **and judgment was given to the saints of the Most High; and the time came that the saints possessed the Kingdom.***

But the judgment shall sit, and they shall take away (from the fourth beast) his dominion, to consume and to destroy it unto the end. And the kingdom and dominion, and the greatness of the kingdom under the whole heaven, shall be given to the people of the saints of the Most High, whose Kingdom is an everlasting Kingdom, and all dominions shall serve and obey Him.

Daniel 7:13-14, 22, 26-27

Now, if Jesus has not yet received the throne and the Father has not yet given us the Kingdom, then the Church has no power and remains in limbo, waiting, which makes no sense.

The author of Hebrews clearly stated that the Kingdom was already ours.

*Therefore, **we receiving a Kingdom which cannot be moved,** let us have grace whereby we may serve God acceptably, with reverence and godly fear.*

Hebrews 12:28

Next, these clouds the prophet Daniel talks about have more to do with the covering that surrounds the throne of the Father than with physical clouds.

Let's look at other cloud concepts in the Word:

2. THE CLOUDS ARE GOD'S TABERNACLE WITH MEN

One of the words translated as cloud in Hebrew is anan, which means *"covering"*, or *"covered sky."*[18]

*Also, can any understand the **spreadings of the clouds (anan)**, or the thundering noise of His tabernacle ?*
Job 36:29

*It is He that sitteth upon the circle of the earth, and the inhabitants thereof are as grasshoppers, who stretcheth out the heavens **as a curtain and spreadeth** them out as a tent to dwell in,...*
Isaiah 40:22

The thundering noise of His tabernacle is the sound of His voice speaking in His dwelling place, which is the congregation of the saints. It's the sound of the cloud of witnesses that make up the eternal temple throughout the ages, it's the sound of the multitude of the saints who make the waters of life flow through worship, each one a stream that joins the other, to form the sound of many waters.

*And I heard, as it were, the voice of a great multitude, and **the voice of many waters, and the voice of***

---

[18] *Strong's Concordance 6051. anan, aw-nawn';* from 6049; a cloud (as covering the sky), i.e. the nimbus or thunder-cloud:—cloud(-y).

163

mighty thunderings, *saying, "Alleluia! For the Lord God Omnipotent reigneth."* *Revelation 19:6*

Therefore, seeing we also are compassed about by so **great a cloud of witnesses,** *let us lay aside every weight, and the sin which doth so easily beset us, and let us run with patience the race that is set before us,...* *Hebrews 12:1*

The clouds represent the anan of God, His Grace covering that protects us.

He made darkness His secret place; His pavilion round about Him was dark waters and thick **clouds of the skies.** *Psalm 18:11*

... who layeth the beams of His chambers in the waters, who maketh **the clouds His chariot,** *who walketh upon the wings of the wind;* *Psalm 104:3*

The clouds are the place from where God speaks to His people, not only in the Old Testament but also in the New; they are symbols of the prophetic manifestation of the Holy Spirit.

While he was saying this, a **cloud** *came and overshadowed them; and they were fearful as they entered the* **cloud.** *And a voice came out of the cloud, saying, "This is My beloved Son, Hear Him!"* *Luke 9:34-35*

*And the LORD descended in the **cloud** and stood with him there, and proclaimed the name of the LORD.*

Exodus 34:5

Then a cloud covered the tent of the congregation, and the glory of the LORD filled the tabernacle. And Moses was not able to enter into the tent of the congregation because the cloud abode thereon, and the glory of the LORD filled the tabernacle.

Exodus 40:34-35

When the **anan** covering of God is removed from a place, the judgments of God are released.

And the heaven departed as a scroll when it is rolled together, and every mountain and island were moved out of their places. And the kings of the earth, and the great men, and the rich men, and the chief captains, and the mighty men, and every bondman, and every free man, hid themselves in the dens and in the rocks of the mountains; and they said to the mountains and rocks, "Fall on us, and hide us from the face of Him that sitteth on the throne, and from the wrath of the Lamb!"

Revelation 6:14-16

This Scripture does not talk about the end of the world, but about how His covering His *anan* is removed so God's righteousness is released over the Earth.

3. THE CLOUDS ARE THE PLACE WHERE HE UNITES WITH HIS PEOPLE

The clouds also symbolize the realm of the Spirit where we become one in Jesus. Another Hebrew word for *cloud* is **chishshur,** which means "unite" and is also the "hub of a wheel" where its spokes unite.[19] The word **chishshur** conveys the idea of the Spirit of the Lord uniting His Body the Church unto Himself.

While Jesus was on Earth, people could only see His phisical body, so no one could be His Body, however, as He manifests Himself in the clouds, He gathers all of us inside of Him to form part of His spiritual Body.

And if I go and prepare a place for you, I will come again and receive you unto Myself, that where I am, there ye may be also. And whither I go ye know, and the way ye know.   *John 14:3-4*

In the Book of Ezekiel, we see how the Spirit of the living creatures moved inside the wheels, in the **chishshur** of God. It's in the **chishshur** where the Spirit of God who gives life and unifies is found.

*Wherever the spirit wanted to go, they went, because there the spirit went; and the **wheels** were lifted together with them, for the spirit of the living creatures was in the **wheels.***   *Ezekiel 1:20*

---

[19] 2840. **rÚ¨vIj chishshur, khish-shoor´;** from an unused root meaning to bind together; combined, i.e. the nave or hub of a wheel (as holding the spokes together):—spoke.

And the glory which Thou gavest Me I have given them,
that they may be one, even as We are one: I in them and
Thou in Me, that they may be made perfect in one, and
that the world may know that Thou hast sent Me and hast
loved them, as Thou hast loved Me. "Father, I will that
*they also, whom Thou hast given Me, **be with Me where***
I am, that they may behold My glory which Thou
***hast given Me;** for Thou loved Me before the foundation*
of the world."   *John 17:22-24*

Jesus sat on His throne and shared His glory with us. We are not separated from the Lord, waiting to go join Him up in the clouds.

If He lives in us and we in Him, we are already eternally united. Where He is, there we also are He came in the Spirit so we would be ONE with the Father and with Him. We are no longer separated from Him.

4. CLOUDS REPRESENT PEOPLE

Jesus comes in the midst of the clouds to judge those who do evil.

These are wells without water, clouds that are carried by
a tempest, for whom the mist of darkness is reserved
forever.   *2 Peter 2:17*

These are spots on your feasts of charity when they feast
*with you, feeding themselves without fear. **Clouds** they*
are without water, carried about by winds; trees whose
fruit withereth, without fruit, twice dead, plucked up by
the roots;   *Jude 1:12*

167

5. CLOUDS REPRESENT TIMES OF JUDGMENT

*That day is a day of wrath, a day of trouble and distress, a day of waste and desolation, a day of darkness and gloominess, a **day of clouds** and thick darkness,*
Zephaniah 1:15

*Behold, he shall come up as **clouds**, and his chariots shall be as a whirlwind. His horses are swifter than eagles! Woe unto us, for we are despoiled!*   *Jeremiah 4:13*

*... a day of darkness and of gloominess, **a day of clouds** and of thick darkness, as the morning spread upon the mountains. A great people and a strong, there hath not been ever the like; neither shall be any more after it, even to the years of many generations.*   *Joel 2:2*

This prophecy is fulfilled when Jesus takes the throne and gives His authority and the Kingdom to the saints of the Most High.

6. EVERY EYE SHALL SEE HIM

*Behold, He cometh with clouds, and **every eye shall see Him,** and they also who pierced Him; and all kindreds of the earth shall wail because of Him. Even so. Amen.*
Revelation 1:7

We see here that in His coming every eye shall see Him. However Jesus told His disciples that He would come in a form the world could not see Him but they would.

Yet a little while and the world seeth Me no more, but ye see Me. Because I live, ye shall live also.
John 14:19

The words *every eye shall see Him* was a Jewish expression that meant something was a fact. It was the same as saying, *it will be evident or it shall be commonly known.* We see this same expression in the book of Isaiah when he prophesied about the glory of God that would come when John the Baptist was to baptize Jesus in the Jordan.

The voice of him that crieth in the wilderness: Prepare ye the way of the LORD; make straight in the desert a highway for our God.
Every valley shall be exalted, and every mountain and hill shall be made low; and the crooked shall be made straight, and the rough places plain.
*And the glory of the LORD shall be revealed, **and all flesh shall see it together;** for the mouth of the LORD hath spoken it.*
Isaiah 40:3-5

When Jesus was baptized, the heavens opened and everybody who was there heard the Father acknowledge the Son:

... and the Holy Ghost descended in a bodily shape like a dove upon Him, and a voice came from Heaven, which said, "THOU ART MY BELOVED SON; IN THEE I AM WELL PLEASED."
Luke 3:22

This was not broadcast via satellite to all the nations; however, it says all flesh jointly saw Him. The disciples and the followers of Jesus recognized that glory, but not the religious folk and those who crucified Him.

Peter talks about another similar moment when they saw the glory of Jehovah during Jesus' transfiguration.

*For we have not followed cunningly devised fables when we made known unto you the power and coming of our Lord Jesus Christ, but **were eyewitnesses of His majesty.** For He received from God the Father honor and glory when there came such a voice to Him from the Excellent Glory: This is My beloved Son, in whom I am well pleased. And this voice, which came from Heaven, we heard when we were with Him on the holy mount.*

2 Peter 1:16-18

When Christ manifests Himself among His people, those who are His disciples see Him. He is the one Who was, Who is, and Who is come, and is constantly coming, or comes in a way that is not related to a precise time, (The greek word **erchomai**[20]) the Almighty, and there are ongoing testimonies of His manifestation through visions i various appearances that occur in the prophetic realm.

How many times do we say: "The Lord is entering the midst of the congregation at this moment", or "we see Him extending His hand and doing miracles"? How many times during warfare

---

[20] ***Strong's Concordance 2064. erchomai;*** middle voice of a primary verb (**used only in the present and imperfect tenses,** the others being supplied by a kindred (middle voice)

The full explanation of this Greek word is found in Instrument 1 of this book.

manifestations do we not see Him coming on His white horse and His angels with Him? How many times have we not seen His arm extended and His brightly shining sword bringing righteousness over a city, or been immersed in an intense cloud of His presence?

There are thousands of believers who have experienced manifestations of this type.

14 MEETING THE LORD IN THE CLOUDS

M y intention is to analyze this subject from a prophetic perspective and from the fundamental principles we have been studying to bring some light that I hope it will bless you.

For the Lord Himself shall descend from Heaven with a shout, with the voice of the archangel and with the trumpet of God; and the dead in Christ shall rise first; then we who are alive and remain shall be caught up together with them in the clouds to meet the Lord in the air. And so shall we ever be with the Lord.
Therefore comfort one another with these words.
1 Thessalonians 4:16-18

I want to first suddivide this subject so it will be easier to understand whar the Apostle Paul was trying to come across.

1. WE ARE ALREADY IN AND WITH THE LORD.

Before attempting to interpret this theme, we have to part from the fact that the heart of the Gospel is that those of us, who already belong to Him, are already eternally united to Him. In Him we live, we move, and have our being (Acts 17:28). In Him we have access to heavenly places, and if He allows us, we can even be caught up into Heaven or be present in front of His throne.

Paul himself, in that same first letter to the *Thessalonians,* tells us how we are already united to Him.

*For God hath not appointed us to wrath, but to obtain salvation by our Lord Jesus Christ who died for us, that, whether we wake or sleep, **we should live together with Him.*** *1 Thessalonians 5:9-10*

The interpretation of this passage where we are snatched away to meet the Lord in the clouds then has to mean something different from a future union with Jesus. I believe it speaks about a personal entering into His presence, a powerful encounter with Jesus in which He genuinely joins His Spirit with ours. In my case, I have had that type of experience many times. The one at the island of *Patmos* was one of them.

2. WHAT DOES IT MEAN TO BE SNATHCED AWAY?

His cloud is real, and to be snatched into it transforms us from glory to glory. Not every person who calls Him "Lord" has this type of experience - only those who have died to their flesh, who love Him and follow Him.

The word clouds in this Scripture is **nephele** in Greek[21] and

---

[21] ***Strong's Concordance 3507. nephele, nef-el'-ay;*** from 3509; properly, cloudiness, i.e. (concretely) a cloud: — cloud.

means "cloudiness." This is the same word used to determine the cloud of witnesses in Hebrews chapter 12.

Paul was talking to the *Thessalonians* regarding the destiny of those who had died in Christ and were already part of the cloud of witnesses and the eternal Body of Christ, and also about the instant transformation of those who were still alive as they were wrapped in His cloud of glory.

Let's remember, they were living in times of great tribulation, waiting for the righteousness of God to manifest itself over their enemy, the *Roman Empire.*

The brethren asked each other what happened to those who died in Christ before He would manifest Himself (referring to the judgment they were awaiting, which would come in the year 70 A.D.)

I believe, by what's been revealed to me, that this scripture refers to Jesus coming to dwell within us. Jesus in His **Chishshur** (cloud-navel of a wheel) joins for Himself His eternal Body and makes us ONE with Him and with the Father. This is in agreement with the words *to catch up* in the first epistle to the Thessalonians, which comes from the word *harpazo* which means "to grab, hold[22]" and is derived from the word *haireomai* which also means to take for oneself.

---

[22] ***Strong Concordance 726. harpazo, har-pad'-zo;*** from a derivative of 138; to seize (in various applications): — catch (away, up), pluck, pull, take (by force).
138. aijreomai, hahee-reh'-om-ahee;. probably akin to 142; to take for oneself, i.e. to prefer: — choose. Some of the forms are borrowed from a cognate **hellomai** which is otherwise obsolete.

Jesus told His disciples that He would come again to take us unto Himself so we could always be with Him. (John 14:1-2) He said He was going to come back to us to make His dwelling place within us. At the moment He comes to our heart, we are transformed thoroughly and are able to hear His voice and to experience His presence inside His cloud of glory. It's when we genuinely are born of the water and of the Spirit that we become like the wind, like the air where He then meets us to direct us by His Spirit. (John 3:6-8)

3. THE CLOUD OF HIS PRESENCE

The cloud of His presence in this case is the word **nephele,** which is the same word used to describe the cloud of witnesses. The **nephele** is the presence of the Lord manifested in a cloud that unites in an instant the believers from every time period, those that were before Christ and those who were alive at that time. This cloud is constantly growing as more and more people join the Lord when they depart from this world.

It was the same "baptism in the cloud" Israel experienced at the time of Moses and which Paul speaks about to the Church.

*Moreover, brethren, I would not have ye ignorant of how all of our fathers were under the cloud, and all passed through the sea, and all were **baptized unto Moses in the cloud** and in the sea. And all ate the same spiritual meat, and all drank the same spiritual drink; for they drank of that spiritual Rock that followed them, and that Rock was Christ.* 1 Corinthians 10:1-4

For the cloud of the LORD was upon the tabernacle by day and fire was on it by night, in the sight of all the house of Israel throughout all their journeys.   Exodus 40:38

This cloud is a type and shadow of the glory of God that rests over the Kingdom believer who is now the tabernacle of God on Earth.

4. RESURRECTED IN OUR SPIRITS

At the sound of His voice, when the revelation of Christ is manifested in our lives, we become conscious that we are one single eternal Body who goes to unite with Him from generation to generation.

In Christ, we are already resurrected in His Kingdom by His Glory to live with the Lord forever and this is what transforms our entire being. Paul knew this and taught it:

If ye then be risen with Christ, seek those things which are above, where Christ sitteth at the right hand of God. Set your affection on things above, not on things on the earth.
*For ye are dead, and your life is hid with Christ in God. When Christ, who is our life, shall appear, (**Phaneroo**-manifest[23]), then shall ye also appear with Him in glory.*
Colossians 3:1-4

---

[23] **Strong Concordance 5319. phaneroo, fan-er-o´-o;** from 5318; to render apparent (literally or figuratively): — appear, manifestly declare, (make) manifest (forth), shew (self).

If our life is hidden in Christ and we are jointly resurrected with Him, that transformation is manifested in our lives. His voice resounds in us like an explosion of resurrection life that continuously quickens us.

This is consistent with what Isaiah said regarding Christ living in us.

Arise, shine, for thy light is come, and the glory of the LORD is risen upon thee. For behold, the darkness shall cover the earth and gross darkness the people; but the LORD shall arise upon thee, and His glory shall be seen upon thee. And the Gentiles shall come to thy light, and kings to the brightness of thy rising.   *Isaiah 60:1-3*

Going back the passage of **1ˢᵗ Thessalonians 4:17**, we see that it is intimately related to **1ˢᵗ Corinthians 15,** where Paul describes the resurrection into a spiritual body of those who are in Jesus.

It is sown a natural body; **it is raised a spiritual body.** *There is a natural body, and there is a spiritual body. And so it is written: "The first man Adam was made a living soul." The last Adam was made* **a quickening Spirit.** *However that which is spiritual was not first, but that which is natural, and afterward that which is spiritual. The first man is of the earth, earthy; the second Man is the Lord from Heaven. As is the earthy, such are they also that are earthy; and* **as is the heavenly, such are they also that are heavenly.** *And as we have borne the image of the earthy, we shall also* **bear the image of the heavenly.** *Now this I say, brethren, that* **flesh** *and blood cannot inherit the Kingdom of God; neither doth corruption inherit incorruption. Behold, I show you a mystery: We shall not all sleep; but we shall all be changed in a moment, in the twinkling of an eye, at the last trumpet. For the trumpet shall sound, and the dead shall be raised incorruptible, and we shall be changed.*

1 Corinthians 15:44-52

Let's note that the passage of 1 Thessalonians 4:16-17 is exactly the same as the last part of these verses in 1 Corinthians 15:

*For the Lord Himself will descend from heaven with a shout, with the voice of an archangel, **and with the trumpet of God. And the dead in Christ will rise first. Then we who are alive and remain shall be caught up** together with them in the clouds to meet the Lord in the air. And thus we shall always be with the Lord.*

1 Thessalonians 4:16-17

Although Paul is certainly talking about the ultimate resurrection of the dead, he is also establishing a principle regarding the transformation undergone by those who are alive and whose spirits have been resurrected in Christ Jesus.

If ye then be risen with Christ, seek those things which are above, where Christ sitteth at the right hand of God

Colossians 3:1

The Church is the image of Christ. In Him we carry the image of the heavenly One. Resurrection starts to be manifested in our lives, while we are still alive, quickening our mortal bodies.

179

Now let's go back to the explanation Paul is giving about transformation when we resurrect in Christ.

The Ressurrection Is Our Heavenly Habitation

For this corruptible must put on incorruption, and this mortal must put on immortality. So when this corruptible **shall have put on incorruption, and this mortal shall have put on immortality,** *then shall be brought to pass the saying that is written:* **"Death is swallowed up in victory."** *1 Corinthians 15:53-54*

We see in this Scripture two things we need to put on: *incorruption and immortality.*

Paul is talking about being genuinely clothed in our heavenly dwelling, which is Christ. Resurrection begins in those who have died in Christ, those who have crucified their desires and passions, while they are still alive in this world.

In his second epistle to the *Corinthians,* Paul again addresses the topic of being clothed in our heavenly dwelling and how to achieve it.

For we know that if our earthly house, this tabernacle, were dissolved, we have a building of God, a house not made with hands, eternal in the heavens. For in this we groan, earnestly desiring to be clothed about with our house which is from Heaven, that, **being so clothed, we shall not be found naked.** *For we that are in this tabernacle do groan, being burdened, not because we*

*would be unclothed, but clothed about, **that mortality might be swallowed up by life.***
2 Corinthians 5:1-4

Paul talks about being found clothed by our heavenly house so all that is mortal could be swallowed up by life. When says "we shall be found clothed," he clearly indicates that he is not referring to something that happens after death, but while we are still alive.

Jesus promised to return spiritually to be our habitation, to make us dwell with Him, to be our resurrection while we're still in this body from now and evermore.

We will not die even though we will leave our earthly bodies behind. We will not go to sleep as it happened to the saints of the Old Covenant. At the moment of parting this world, we will instantaneously be in His Presence completely alive; we will only be divested of our flesh.

*... O death, where is thy sting? O grave, where is thy victory? The sting of death is sin, and the strength of sin is the law. But thanks be to God, who **giveth us the victory** through our Lord Jesus Christ!*
1 Corinthians 15:55-57

This verse is key for us to realize that Paul talks about the effectiveness of the resurrection dwelling in us.

"But concerning the dead, that they rise: have ye not read in the book of Moses, how in the bush God spoke unto him, saying, "I am the God of Abraham, and the God of

*Isaac, and the God of Jacob"? He is not the God of the
dead, but the God of the living. Ye therefore do greatly
err."* Mark 12:26-27

5. HIS MANIFESTATION IN OUR MIDST

Jesus also talked about how the manifestation of His presence
(**parousia**[24]) would be. He was talking to those who would enter
great persecution in their time. He needed to encourage them in
the face of the approaching tribulation.

*"I will not leave you comfortless; **I will come to you.** Yet
a little while and the world seeth Me no more, **but ye see
Me.** Because I live, ye shall live also.   At that day ye shall
know that I am in My Father, and you in Me, and I in you.
He that hath My commandments and keepeth them, he it
is that loveth Me; and he that loveth Me shall be loved by
My Father, and I will love him and will **manifest Myself
to him."** Judas (not Iscariot) said unto Him, "Lord, how
is it that **Thou wilt manifest Thyself unto us,** and not
unto the world?"*
*Jesus answered and said unto him, "If a man loves Me, he
will keep My words; and My Father will love him, and **We
will come unto him and make Our abode with him.***
John 14:18-23

---

[24] ***Strong Concordance 3952. parousia, par-oo-see'-ah***; from the present participle of
3918; a being near, i.e. advent (often, return; specially, of Christ to punish Jerusalem, or
finally the wicked); (by implication) physically, aspect: — coming, presence.
3918. pareimi, par'-i-mee; from 3844 and 1510 (including its various forms); to be near,
i.e. at hand; neuter present participle (singular) time being, or (plural) property: — come,
x have, be here, + lack, (be here) present.
Full description of the word can be found in Instrument 1 of this book.

We see here once again how the covering of His tabernacle is the key to His manifestation. He returned to them, He did not leave them comfortless, and they saw Him because He made His abode with them as He does with us.

This coming back to indwell those who love Him is obviously not the *second coming*.

According to what we have been studying *Jesus coming in the clouds* has to do with His manifestation as King of kings governing and ruling Earth with all believers. This implies that this transformation happens when His voice, which sounds like a trumpet, reveals in us the glorified Christ who quickens our spirit. Trumpets are symbols of the prophetic voice. In an instant our dormant spirit is brought to life to see and hear the Kingdom of God.

> *I was in the Spirit on the Lord's Day, and I heard behind me a great voice as of a trumpet, saying, "I am Alpha and Omega, the First and the Last," and, "What thou seest, write in a book and send it unto the seven churches which are in Asia ..."*   *Revelation 1:10 and 11a*

John heard the trumpet and gives us the example of how the revelation of His glory progresses in the life of a believer, opening up for him/her the heavenly dimensions.

A nd Jesus said unto them, "Verily I say unto you, that ye that have followed Me, in the regeneration when the Son of Man shall sit on the throne of His glory, ye also shall sit upon twelve thrones, judging the twelve tribes of Israel." *Matthew 19:28*

As we have seen throughout this book, Jesus grants the saints the faculty to judge. He opened the way so that as His saints we can boldly enter before the throne and once inside, watch how Heaven is organized to release Judgment. It is the man-child of the *Book of Revelation,* Chapter 12, who has access to Heaven to judge with the rod of iron.

And she brought forth a man-child, who was to rule all nations with a rod of iron: and her child was caught up unto God, and to His throne. *Revelation 12:5*

This man-child represents the overcoming believers who have denied their life unto death; the ones who learned to wrestle against the devil and subject him under their feet. There are always words of triumph in their mouth to remind satan of all the ways they have defeated him. These are the words of their testimony.

And they overcame him by the blood of the Lamb and by the word of their testimony, and they did not love their lives to the death. Revelation 12:11

1. THE 24 ELDERS

Once we overcome in every commandment found in the seven letters that Jesus gave to the churches in Asia, we are then ready to understand the **Supreme Court of Heaven** and its judgments. Overcoming establishes our position and opens the doors of Heaven for us. This is the *nineth basic theme of interpretation.*

The Apostle John, a first fruit of that overcoming Church, is raptured into Heaven (like many are nowadays) to see and be part of God's amazing government design prepared for His Church.

Note that John was at one level *in the spirit* (in Chapter1) and then in Chapter 4 he enters into a higher and deeper level of this experience. He moves from the level of *Revelation* into the level of *Government.*

I was in the Spirit on the Lord's Day, and heard behind me a great voice, as of a trumpet, Revelation 1:10

After this I looked, and, behold, a door was opened in Heaven: and the first voice which I heard was as it were of a trumpet talking with me; which said, Come up hither, and I will shew thee things which must be hereafter.

186

And immediately I was in the spirit: and, behold, a throne was set in Heaven, and One sat on the throne.

Revelation 4:1-2

Revelation is granted through intimacy and the pursuit of God, but rulership comes only by overcoming the system of *Babylon*. There is a type of authority granted unto us by grace as part of our redemption; however, there is another one that is conquered. In the Kingdom of God, Heaven and Earth operate jointly.

Around the throne in Heaven, there are 24 elders and four cherubim or living creatures. Twenty-four is the number of perfect government; it's the divine design Jesus gave His Church to govern and judge: she is part of His Supreme Court of Justice

And He that sat was to look upon like a jasper and a sardius stone: and there was a rainbow round about the throne, in sight like unto an emerald.
*And round about the throne were **four and twenty seats:** and upon the seats **I saw four and twenty elders** sitting, clothed in white raiment; and they had on their heads crowns of gold.*   *Revelation 4:3-4*

This is the model Jesus left us to be a victorious, heavenly-directed, living organism; the Church built up by Him, against whom the gates of hell cannot prevail.

The elders are called by this name since they manifest the character of God. We see in the book of *Daniel* the Father is called by a term having the same meaning: *Ancient*. His throne is fire, since this is the element that symbolizes His judgments.

187

I beheld till the thrones were cast down, and the Ancient of Days sat down, whose garment was white as snow and the hair of His head like the pure wool. His throne was like the fiery flame, and His wheels as burning fire.
A fiery stream issued and came forth from before Him. Thousand thousands ministered unto Him, and ten thousand times ten thousand stood before Him: the judgment was set, and the books were opened.

Daniel 7: 9-10

*... until the **Ancient of Days** came, and judgment was given to the saints of the Most High; and the time came that the saints possessed the Kingdom...*   *Daniel 7:22*

And I saw thrones and they that sat upon them, and judgment was given unto them...   *Revelation 20:4a*

These 24 elders were not people John could recognize. They are certainly not the twelve tribes of *Israel,* and neither are they the twelve apostles as individuals, but as a representation of Church government. John is not seeing himself or his fellow apostles upon any of the elder's thrones.

This number is symbolic and represents the divine structure of government in every nation and in every city of the world.

*And they sung a new song, saying, Thou art worthy to take the book, and to open the seals thereof: for thou wast slain, and **hast redeemed us to God by thy blood out of every kindred, and tongue, and people, and nation;***

And hast made us unto our God kings and priests: and
we shall reign on the earth.   *Revelation 5:9-10*

Understanding the place of elders is key in the Kingdom of God. Today, when we talk about elders in the Church, we think of them as the group of leaders under a senior pastor, but this was never intended to be this way.

Elders are the key component to bring the Kingdom of God into the Earth. As Paul established churches during his travels, he assigned elders over cities and not pastors over congregations.

For this cause left I thee in Crete, that thou shouldest set
in order the things that are wanting, and ordain elders in
every city, as I had appointed thee: *Titus 1:5*

Elders have a burden and a comprehension about their city and also about their God-given authority to rule over it alongside other elders. They don't think in terms of *my* congregation or *my* network, but in terms of God's Kingdom being established in every area of society within the city and how they are responsible to make it happen as a team.

God has to reposition men and women into the right places where He has called them to minister. The whole structure of the Church has to be lined up with His designs, not with those we have inherited from *Babylon* in the sixteenth century. For this to happen, He has already started a major reformation of heavenly and prophetic understanding so we can rule and reign with Him under His terms and not under ours. This is not about destroying churches and pastors. He is reforming them into a new

189

understanding so we can all walk as ONE Church in the victory and the power He has given us.

Many of those functioning as apostles, prophets, and pastors will be repositioned by God to function within His system of justice.

a) God Wants Elders in The World Today

As we can see in this heavenly design, elders are overcomers over *Babylon*. They have been promoted to constantly be around the throne. They understand true worship which is what keeps them in this very close position to God. They move deeply in the prophetic dimension of Heaven to grab hold of what Heaven is saying at all times. It is from this understanding and knowledge of Heaven that they can properly rule over the earth.

They have entered a level of God's glory only granted to those who have been able to understand God's judgments and the way He establishes His justice. In this level we see four living creatures, which are the cherubs that move and operate within the glory of God; it's the Glory of His righteousness that judges everything that opposes Him.

And before the throne there was a sea of glass like unto crystal: and in the midst of the throne, and round about the throne, were four beasts full of eyes before and behind. And the first beast was like a lion, and the second beast like a calf, and the third beast had a face as a man, and the fourth beast was like a flying eagle. And the four beasts had each of them six wings about him; and they

190

were full of eyes within: and they rest not day and night,
saying, Holy, holy, holy, Lord God Almighty, Who was,
and is, and is to come.   *Revelation 4:6-8*

They are full of eyes because they see every circumstance from every possible angle in order to judge according to God's wisdom.

The Elders are in agreement with the four living creatures (cherubs) who let them know *how* to judge and rule from Heaven down to Earth.

Each one of these cherubs has been given a different perspective of God's judgments. The lion sees from the point of view of God the King; the calf, from the eyes of Jesus the servant; the man, from His overcoming humanity; and the eagle from the wisdom of an uplifted spirit, viewing from the perspective of Heaven.

A biblical case of this manner of judging is shown in how God dealt with His servant Paul of *Tarsus*. On one end he was a murderer, but on the other end he had the zeal of God, and with great boldness he endeavored to accomplish what he erroneously deemed was God's will. God did not judge him solely for his wrongness; instead, He saw what was favorable in his character and transformed him into a great apostle.

Both the living creatures and the elders are constantly acknowledging the headship, the sovereignty and the glory of God. They always aim to exalt God's achievements never man's.

The elders display their authentic humility by casting down their crowns so the exaltation only goes to the Lord and not to themselves. What is important for them is their position around the throne not that their names are known. They are not pursuing fame or to have the largest crowd or the biggest church, although they may have that. They never want to lose their place and their heavenly function. They are not in competition with one another, but in agreement and fellowship because they all hear the same things coming from the throne. They spend time together so they can all experience and hear the instructions from God in order to be accurate in their judgments and counsel.

The throne of God can be seen from many characteristics and many angles. In Chapters 4 and 5 of the *Book of Revelation,* the ones being manifested are *righteousness and judgment.* The 24 elders are immersed in the midst of God's powerful presence that produces thunder and lightning similar to what Moses saw in *Mount Sinai,* as he was approaching the terrible Presence of God to receive the Law. The mountain was smoking with thunder and fire surrounding its summit. He was receiving the authority to rule, to counsel and to release the judgments of God. Moses was face to face with God's glory in the same manner as we see the 24 Elders before the throne.

And out of the throne proceeded lightnings and thunderings and voices: and there were seven lamps of fire burning before the throne, which are the seven Spirits of God.
Revelation 4:5

The seven spirits are in the midst of them because the Elders rule with the understanding of the fullness of the Spirit. In Chapter 5 of the *Book of Revelation* we see the One on the throne holding a scroll that none in Heaven or Earth could open, and John is saddened because of this. We clearly see here the operation of Heaven before the *First Coming* of Christ and after His ascension. Before Messiah came, no one could release God's judgments. It's the Elders who are around the glory - those who see Jesus as King in His full authority, the ones who are able to bring this revelation to the Body of Christ represented by John here.

> *And one of the elders saith unto me, Weep not: behold, the Lion of the tribe of Judah, the Root of David, hath prevailed to open the book, and to loose the seven seals thereof. And I beheld, and, lo, in the midst of the throne and of the four beasts, and in the midst of the elders, stood a Lamb as it had been slain, having seven horns and seven eyes, which are the seven Spirits of God sent forth into all the earth.* Revelation 5:5-6

The elders have the power to release from Heaven the authority of the *Lion of Judah* and a deep revelation of the cross that will execute the judgments of the Lamb.

Until the elders reveal this aspect of Messiah, the Church (John) is able to see the Lamb upon the throne next to the Father. This is not just talking about the Lamb being enthroned in external terms, but instead, in having a true knowledge of this fact in our innermost being.

> ***And I beheld, and, lo, in the midst of the throne*** and of the four beasts, and in the midst of the elders, stood a Lamb as it had been slain ... Revelation 5:6a

John is beholding the transition between God's government in the Old Testament - The Father seated at His throne - and Jesus in

193

His Kingdom seated at the throne with His Father, which includes the saints, through the structure of eldership in the New Covenant.

Notice the difference between Chapter 1 and Chapter 5 in the **Book of Revelation**. In Chapter 1, representing the old government, the Father is upon the throne and the seven Spirits are before Him. In Chapter 5 we see the newrulership, The Father and the Lamb are merged on the throne, and the seven Spirits are **within** Jesus.

Elders see the Lamb beyond the bounds of salvation as the One now sitting on the throne and possessing the full manifestation of the Holy Spirit. This is the core of their message and the way they manifest God's presence to the Church.

They see and point us to Jesus so we can see Him in all His power and in all the manifold wisdom and knowledge of the true baptism of the Spirit.

The Church needs the rising up of the elders who see Jesus on His throne and can say BEHOLD! ...opening up the eyes of the believers to see Him as He really is in His glory and Authority.

Another important characteristic of Elders is their passion to worship God.

And when He had taken the book, the four living beings and the four and twenty elders fell down before the Lamb, having every one of them harps and golden vials full of incense, which are the prayers of saints.

Revelation 5:8

194

The heavenly harps given to the elders are the revelation of prophetic worship. They understand the sounds of Heaven and the new songs in order to bring them down to the Earth.

Elders bring the atmosphere of God into a place through their worship. This type of adoration is directed by the Holy Spirit and has nothing to do with our beautifully written songs; it's a new song. As they bring the realm of Heaven down, the prayers of the saints are activated before the Throne.

There is a close relationship between the harps and the vials of incense.

It is not the function of the elders to only pray for the needs of the Body, making people dependent on them, lazy and ignorant. Instead, they teach people how to pray, and through their worship and position before the throne they add power to their prayers. I don't mean by this that they do not pray for the people - they do – because they know the heart of the Father, who yearns to bless His beloved. We see this same effect in Chapter 8.

And another angel came and stood at the altar, having a golden censer; and there was given unto him much incense, that he should offer it with the prayers of all saints upon the golden altar, which was before the throne. And the smoke of the incense, which came with the prayers of the saints, ascended up before God out of the angel's hand. And the angel took the censer, and filled it with fire from the altar, and cast it onto the earth; and there were voices and thunderings and lightnings, and an earthquake. *Revelation 8:3-5*

Elders are also assigned by God to bring forth the revelation of the heavenly reality to the believers. They exercise an apostolic ability to make Heaven real and to establish the promises of God among His people.

Then, addressing me, one of the elders [of the Heavenly Sanhedrin] said, Who are these [people] clothed in the long white robes? And from where have they come?
I replied, Sir, you know. And he said to me, These are they who have come out of the great tribulation (persecution), and have washed their robes and made them white in the blood of the Lamb.
For this reason they are [now] before the [very] throne of God and serve Him day and night in His sanctuary (temple); and He Who is sitting upon the throne will protect and spread His tabernacle over and shelter them with His presence.
They shall hunger no more, neither thirst any more; neither shall the sun smite them, nor any ascorching heat.
For the Lamb Who is in the midst of the throne will be their Shepherd, and He will guide them to the springs of the waters of life; and God will wipe away every tear from their eyes. Revelation 7:13-17 AMP

As I previously stated, the saints referred to in this chapter are not those who are already dead, but those who are still alive on Earth. That is why He shepherds them and leads them to the living waters. In Heaven they don't need protection, nor are they in a desert needing water.

The elders reveal to the Church (John) the position and the

power of those who overcome their trials. Because elders live worshipping before the throne, they can bring words from Heaven to encourage the believers. They don't feed the people, but make sure that the Lamb feeds them and quenches their thirst. They lead the Church to serve before the throne and not to serve around a man.

b) The Church Receives The Faculty To Judge

Besides the elders, the angels and the archangels appear before the throne to carry out the sentences of the Most High and convey them to the saints so they can decree His judgments cause them to come to pass.

*This matter is by the decree of the watchers, and **the demand by the word of the holy ones,** with the intent that the living may know that the Most High ruleth in the kingdom of men, and giveth it to whomsoever He will, and setteth up over it the basest of men.*
Daniel 4:17

*... until the Ancient of Days came, and **judgment was given to the saints of the Most High;** and the time came that the saints possessed the Kingdom.*
Daniel 7:22

*... saying, "Hurt not the earth, neither the sea nor the trees, **till we have sealed the servants of our God in their foreheads."***   *Revelation 7:3*

Who are these chosen ones? These are the ones who are with

Him and follow Him wherever He goes.

"These shall make war with the Lamb, and the Lamb shall overcome them; for He is Lord of lords and King of kings, and they that are with Him are called, and are chosen, and faithful." Revelation 17:14

The number of the Chosen is symbolic and is 144.000. They are represented as 12 000 from each of the Israli tribes. This is a prophetic number that symbolizes all the saints from every time period Jews and gentiles together. Twelve represents goverment. 12 times 12, equals 144, portrais the manifested Kingdom or God's Supreme Government. 1,000 symbolizes the countless, hundreds of thousands, like the number of the stars or the sand

*"... were born as many as the **stars** of the sky in multitude innumerable as the **sand** which is by the seashore.*
Hebrews 11:12b

And they sang, as it were, a new song before the throne, and before the four living beings and the elders; and no man could learn that song, except the hundred and forty and four thousand who were redeemed from the earth. These are they that were not defiled with women, for they are virgins. These are they that follow the Lamb whithersoever He goeth. These were redeemed from among men, being the firstfruits unto God and to the Lamb. And in their mouth was found no guile, for they are without fault before the throne of God.
Revelation 14:3-5

Some examples of the number 1,000 in the Bible are:

And the women answered one another as they played, and said, "Saul hath slain his thousands, and David his ten thousands." 1 Samuel 18:7

1,000 also symbolizes that which is perfect:
10 x 10 x 10 = 1,000, meaning Heaven itself.

Then I looked, and I heard the voices of many angels on every side of the throne and of the living creatures and the elders [of the Heavenly Sanhedrin], and they numbered ten thousand times ten thousand and thousands of thousands... Revelation 5:11 AMP

After this I looked and a vast host appeared which no one could count, [gathered out] of every nation, from all tribes and peoples and languages. These stood before the throne and before the Lamb; they were attired in white robes, with palm branches in their hands.
Revelation 7:9

The chosen ones are in continuous contact with the prophetic, and they worship according to Heaven's worship, which is why they have a new song. They have washed their garments in the blood of the Lamb and are the true tabernacle of God on Earth. The dwelling place of God is above every tribulation: those who dwell herein have laid hold of everything Jesus has conquered at the cross of Calvary and drink from the living waters of the Lamb.

16 GOD'S JUDGMENTS

T he LORD reigneth, let the earth rejoice! Let the multitude of isles be glad thereof! Clouds and darkness are round about Him; righteousness and judgment are the habitation of His throne. A fire goeth before Him, and burneth up His enemies round about. His lightnings enlightened the world; the earth saw and trembled. The hills melted like wax at the presence of the LORD, at the presence of the Lord of the whole earth. The Heavens declare His righteousness, and all the people see His glory. *Psalm 97:1-6*

Along with the previous chapter, this is our last basic theme of interpretation to know God as supreme judge of the universe.

Although the Earth has been under the power of darkness, the ONLY sovereign God has always been Jehovah. The devil is not an authority, nor does he understand government. These are attributes that only God has, and those to whom He gives them.

He has reigned throughout the centuries executing righteousness and judgment over all the nations. He is slow to anger and abounding in mercy, but on the day He acts, His judgments are manifested.

1. THE DAY OF THE LORD

God's time is different from ours.

But, beloved, be not ignorant of this one thing: that with the Lord one day is as a thousand years, and a thousand years as one day. 2 *Peter 3:8*

In general, the interpretation given to the expressions the *Lord's day or the day of the vengeance of our God* has been the end of all things.

On one end, futurist theologians associated this "day" with the "Great Tribulation" in which the seals, trumpets, and vials of the *Apocalypse (the Book of Revelation)* are poured out over a latter generation, which is the one receiving the accumulated wrath of God. This would make God an unjust judge. Why would one single generation have to pay for the atrocities the world has committed throughout the centuries? The total, final "end of the world " as we know it, is also attributed to this day.

The reality is that it has nothing to do with a particular day, or with one period or with two periods. Instead, it symbolizes *each* time period when Jehovah has released, and will release, His wrath.

Allow me to explain this thoroughly. The first thing we need to understand is that there was an imminent judgment that Jesus predicted over Old Covenant *Israel* and over the *Jerusalem* of His time. As we saw before, there is a clear division in Scripture between the ancient world or era, and the new.

*"The Spirit of the Lord GOD is upon Me, because the LORD hath anointed Me.... To proclaim the acceptable year of the LORD, and **the day of vengeance of our God; ...**"*
Isaiah 61:1a and 2a

In this passage Isaiah uses the word year to determine a period of grace for the preaching of the Gospel IN ISRAEL. Until the day of His ascension, the ministry of Jesus was solely to the Jews. It was His people who He warned about how one day He would return (spiritually) to judge *Israel,* thereby destroying the temple and the ancient priestly and sacrificial system.

With the crucifixion, the cup of wrath was filled to the brim. *Jerusalem* had been the city that killed all the prophets of God and finally ended the life of the Messiah.

Jesus' death unleashed a time period referred to as the *wrath of God* on the heavenly clock. By His grace the Father granted a time of patience so the gospel could be preached and a large amount of the people from that generation could be saved. In the scripture we just read Isaiah that called that time period *the acceptable year of the Lord.*

The Lord is not slack concerning his promise, as some men count slackness; but is longsuffering to us-ward, not willing that any should perish, but that all should come to repentance.
2 Peter 3:9

That patience necessarily had to refer to the generation living at that time, since it is possible to increase the number of believers in one generation and to decreasse the number of people being lost; this is not true for the sum total of generations.

If we extend this period of patience to countless numbers of generations century after century, the margin of lost souls would increase since more people are born into the world than those who are saved in each generation.

Let's think about this using this small mathematical formula: every 40 years, symbol of a generation, millions of people go to hell. There are nations at this precise moment that have less than a 1% of Christians. Despite the stunning growth of the gospel during these last decades, we are not even 5% of the world population.

If Jesus' longsuffering refers to waiting throughout the centuries for fewer people to become lost, the Christian population today would have to be 90% of humanity. Then the wait would be worthy. On the contrary, history shows that the Earth has lived practically in darkness from the second century until now.

If the *day of the Lord* announced by the prophets and the apostles was soon to happen in our days, God would lose the battle, since the devil would take the majority of humanity to hell.

Jesus was talking about the judgment coming over the generation of His days. To love them and prepare them, He sent His Holy Spirit so everyone could have the opportunity to be saved.

In Chapters 2 and 3 of Joel, the Lord talks about the impressive manifestation of His grace sent before the judgment of the years 66 to 70 A.D.

There are many other passages that also refer to Messiah's Grace being poured throughout *Israel*, described as brooks and streams of water revitalizing the dry land.

And upon every high mountain and upon every high hill there will be brooks and streams of water in the day of the great slaughter [the day of the Lord], when the towers fall [and all His enemies are destroyed].

Isaiah 30:25 AMP

Of course, the Holy Spirit is available to every person throughout generations and His grace towards us never ends nor do His wells of living water end either.

2. THE LANGUAGE OF GOD CONCERNING HIS JUDGMENTS

God's expressions and manner of speech many times differ from ours. For example, when God uses expressions such as "the heavens shall roll up as a scroll, the stars shall fall from their place, the sun and the moon shall shine no more," or "the Earth shall forever be desolate and never again shall the son of man inhabit it," we think about the end of the world; but God here is referring to a judgment, - one of great magnitude.

We see this clearly when the prophets Isaiah, Jeremiah, Ezekiel, Amos, and Obadiah prophesy *Edom's* total destruction. If we interpret it literally it appears that Jehovah will erase it from the map. However, today that land corresponds to the beautiful land of Jordan with godly churches in it (Jeremiah.49:33, Book of Revelation 6:13-14, Isaiah 34:2-4 y 8-10).

We see the same expressions of total destruction on the "day of the Lord's wrath" when Isaiah predicts judgment over ancient *Babylon*. This prophecy was fulfilled when the Medes and the Persians conquered it.

Behold, the day of the LORD cometh, cruel, both with wrath and fierce ang er, to lay the land desolate; and He shall destroy the sinners thereof out of it. *For the stars of Heaven and the constellations thereof shall not give their light; the sun shall be darkened in his going forth, and the moon shall not cause her light to shine.* *And I will punish the world for their evil and the wicked for their iniquity; and I will cause the arrogance of the proud to cease, and will lay low the haughtiness of the terrible. I will make a man more precious than fine gold, even a man than the golden wedge of Ophir. Therefore* ***I will shake the Heavens, and the earth shall remove out of her place,*** *in the wrath of the LORD of hosts and in the day of His fierce anger. "Behold, I will stir up* **the Medes** *against them, who shall not regard silver; and as for gold, they shall not delight in it.*

Isaiah 13: 9-13, 17

The Earth was not destroyed; neither was it removed from its place, yet *Babylon* was conquered by the Medes and Persians, the second heaven was shaken and the *Babylonian* system of those days was crushed. Malachi also prophesied like Isaiah regarding the *coming of the Lord* as a "day of judgment," not to destroy His people but to refine them.

> **But who may abide the day of His coming?** And who shall stand when He appeareth? For He is like a refiner's fire and like fullers' soap. And He shall sit as a refiner and purifier of silver; and He shall purify the sons of Levi, and purge them as gold and silver, that they may offer unto the LORD an offering in righteousness.
>
> Malachi 3:2-3

God, in His greatness and righteousness will not pour out the full burning of His wrath over one single last generation that would be unjust. The generation of our time is full of abominations and is undoubtedly attracting God's judgments upon themselves; however, each generation and every nation have also felt them.

3. THE JUDGMENTS IN THE BOOK OF REVELATION

If we understand that God is righteous for every era and for every kindred, then we will realize that the **Book of Revelation** is the revelation of Jesus as a governing Judge. To govern is to judge and to establish righteousness.

The judgments and plagues in this book are centered against a spiritual government called *Babylon.* This is the evil empire's main structure, as we studied before.

In a spiritual sense, *Babylon* was established over the Jerusalem of Jesus' time. The whole religious system had been corrupted and was reaching its end. Its sins resembled *Egypt's* and its spiritual fornication equaled *Sodom's*.

> *And their dead bodies shall lie in the street of the great city, which spiritually is called **Sodom and Egypt, where also our Lord was crucified.*** Revelation 11:8

> *And the woman whom thou sawest is that great city which reigneth over the kings of the earth.*
> Revelation 17:18

Jesus appeared to John initially to declare to him the judgment coming over *Jerusalem* and over the spiritual *Babylonian* empire that had overtaken her.

In all the passages where we see the seals, woes, trumpets, and vials, we see a description of the judgment of the old system and the fall of the old *Jerusalem;* thereafter, we see the revelation of God's judgments throughout all time periods. He displays Himself to John as the One Who is, Who was, and Who comes (erchomai, This word is found in the original manuscripts in a grammatical tense called *aoristo*). This tense does not exist in Spanish or English. It is not future, but a punctual time, undefined and timeless, not related to any time frame.

Many Roman emperors subdued *Israel* in great tribulation. *Jerusalem* was besieged and destroyed in the year 70 A.D., and hose who were able to flee to the mountains saved their lives. (See Instrument 2)

4.- JUDGMENTS THROUGHOUT HISTORY

And I saw, and behold a white horse: and he that sat on him had a bow; and a crown was given unto him: and he went forth conquering, and to conquer.

And there went out another horse that was red: and power was given to him that sat thereon to take peace from the earth, and that they should kill one another: and there was given unto him a great sword.

And when he had opened the third seal, I heard the third beast say, Come and see. And I beheld, and lo a black horse; and he that sat on him had a pair of balances in his hand.

And I looked, and behold a pale horse: and his name that sat on him was Death, and Hell followed with him. And power was given unto them over the fourth part of the earth, to kill with sword, and with hunger, and with death, and with the beasts of the earth.

Revelation 6:2, 4-5, 8

God's judgments have been released throughout the ages. I believe the white horse represents the believers who have received the faculty to judge: the overcomers that are coming out to establish God's judgments over the Earth. The red horse, the symbol of *death and war,* has been released many times throughout history, likewise the black one that represents *shortages and famine* and the pale one that releases *sickness and plagues.*

Earthquakes, tsunamis, hurricanes, tornadoes, merciless fires, hail, and financial crisis are all forms of how God judges the nations; sometimes it's to bring conviction of sin and repentance;

at other times, it's to severely punish the iniquity and arrogance of men.

Other judgments include the terrible plagues and epidemics that have scourged humanity. During the bubonic plague of the Middle Ages, also called *Black Death,* people cried out wanting to die because of the pain and the brokenness from this disease. A third of the world population died in 1918 during the Spanish influenza. AIDS is a clear judgment of God against sexual aberrations.

The number of dead people, congenital malformations, and organ destruction caused by vaccines and the side effects of pharmaceutical drugs is yet another form of judgment, in which God allows men to suffer the consecuences of their own choices.

I personally had a vision about the **Book of Revelation,** Chapter 9, where I saw millions of demons coming out from the abyss with syringes (stings) in their hands and forcing substances upon people, which would damage their organs with great pain. Spiritually they wore golden crowns, which are the exaltation of the scientific mind, and their faces were like me.

They appeared humanitarian but were murderers. They made much noise with their lying advertisements on TV and through every media source, making people addicted to medication they never required or that would not heal them either. They had breastplates, they were protected by governments and insurance companies. Their end is not to heal but to destroy, because its leader is Apollyon, the destroyer. And I saw how God judged those who put their trust science, on not on Him.[25]

Another way of judgment is through unrighteous and stern governments. God has allowed tyrant kings and dictators to subdue people. In the Old Covenant He turned *Israel* over to be enslaved by *Egypt,* then by *Babylon,* and then persecuted by *Assyria.* He also allowed unjust judges and wicked kings to govern over them to teach them repentance and faithfulness to Him.

In the Christian era we have seen these same tyrants full of wickedness such as Hitler, Mussolini, Stalin, Saddam Hussein, Fidel Castro, and others. These are persons dominated by an unrelenting thirst to dominate the world, ruled by satan himself, to kill and destroy and govern by terrible oppression.

The seals, trumpets, and vials of the **Book of Revelation** are diverse ways that God judges the Earth, not as one major event, but repeatedly throughout history.

5. ANGELS INTERACT WITH THE CHURCH TO BRING FORTH THE JUDGMENTS OF GOD.

We see all throughout the **Book of Revelation** the existing relationship between the angels and John they reveal things to him, and they transfer him from one place to another in the heavenly dimensions and in the regions where the great powers of darkness live and act.

In Chapter 10 we see an angel giving John a little book to eat,

---

[25] A full understanding of this subject, is found in my book *Pharamakeia, The Assassin of Health.*

and, after doing so, John is given the mandate to prophesy to every tongue and nation.

And I took the little book out of the angel's hand and ate it up, and it was in my mouth sweet as honey; and as soon as I had eaten it, my belly was bitter.
And he said unto me, **"Thou must prophesy again before many peoples and nations, and tongues and kings."** *Revelation 10: 10 - 11*

Historically this never happened; there is no evidence that John traveled everywhere taking a message. This, therefore, speaks to us either as a symbol of the Church receiving the prophetic word and taking it to every nation, or as John's spirit, in the same manner as Elijah's spirit bringing us the mysteries of God.

The Spirit of prophecy is determinant in understanding the dimensions of the Spirit. It's within this realm where the Church is being trained to rule and to understand how and when to loose a judgment that has come from the throne of God.

I want to make it clear that the Judgments of God cannot be released by just any Christian, but by the elders, the apostles and prophets that form the system of justice of the Kingdom of God.

6. JUDGMENTS PROMPT THE BATTLES OF HEAVEN

Every spiritual battle we fight on Earth has a judgment at its core. During these, we see how an army of angels fights alongside the Church. Many times Michael is the one heading an important battle.

212

They fight in the invisible spheres, but God gives us the title of "battle overcomers."

And there was war in Heaven: Michael and his angels fought against the dragon; and the dragon fought and his angels, And they (the saints) overcame him by the blood of the Lamb and by the word of their testimony, and they loved not their lives unto the death.

Revelation 12:7, 11

I have commanded My sanctified ones; I have also called My mighty ones for Mine anger, even them that rejoice in My highness." They come from a far country, from the end of Heaven, even the LORD and the weapons of His indignation, to destroy the whole land.

Isaiah 13:3.5

7. DIVERSE ANGELS IN THE BOOK OF REVELATION

Angels are our fellow servants and work with us in many forms. When somebody receives the authority from God to legislate from Heaven and to fight next to the Lamb, all these angels will be at their disposition.

We see in the **Book of Revelation** diverse types of angelical messengers. Learning about them helps us to pray and loose them according to the leading of the Spirit.

Getting to know angels is a two-edged weapon. There have been many cases in history where Christians received angelical visitations and ended up worshipping them or depending on

213

them more than from God, facing sudden destruction afterwards. The outstanding beauty and power of certain angels is sometimes hard to handle, even John the apostle fell at the feet of an angel and was going to worship him.

And I fell at his feet to worship him. But he said to me, "See that you do not do that! I am your fellow servant, and of your brethren who have the testimony of Jesus. Worship God! For the testimony of Jesus is the spirit of prophecy." Revelation 19:10

Some may ask, "Why do we need angels, if we have the Holy Spirit operating through us?" Angels are like voltage regulators of the glory of God. Some messages, we receive them directly from the realm of God's glory, will simply scorch us. The Apostle John was undoubtedly Spirit-filled; however, he received the message of the **Book of Revelation** through the angel of Jesus Christ.

Judgment Angels

They are in charge of executing the judgments of the seals, vials, trumpets, the earthquakes, the plagues and other forms of judgment and have done this throughout history.

Angels of the 4 Winds

These are in charge of everything that has to do with winds. They can either loose them or stop them. In this next Scripture they are restraining them, but this is not their only assignment in eternity.

And after these things I saw four angels standing on the four corners of the earth, holding the four winds of the earth, that the wind should not blow on the earth, nor on the sea, nor on any tree. Revelation 7:1

The Angel of the Eternal Gospel

This is an angel that has been active throughout the ages. I believe even in the Old Testament when the gospel was preached (Hebrews 4:2), he was there operating from the invisible dimensions. Today, we can also release him to bring revival to our cities.

For unto us was the gospel preached, as well as unto them: but the word preached did not profit them, not being mixed with faith in them that heard it.
Hebrews 4:2

*And I saw another angel fly in the midst of Heaven, having the everlasting **gospel** to preach unto them that dwell on the earth, and to every nation, and kindred, and tongue, and people...* Revelation 14:6

Angels of Incense

And another angel came and stood at the altar, having a golden censer; and there was given unto him much incense, that he should offer it with the prayers of all saints upon the golden altar, which was before the throne.
Revelation 8:3

Angels of Glory

And after these things, I saw another angel come down from Heaven, having great power; and the earth was lightened by his glory. Revelation 18:1

Angels who Carry Out Prophetic Acts From Heaven

Then a mighty angel took up a stone like a great millstone, and cast it into the sea, saying, "Thus with violence shall that great city Babylon be thrown down, and shall be found no more at all..." Revelation 18:21

Jailer Angels, God's Police

And I saw an angel come down from Heaven, having the key to the bottomless pit and a great chain in his hand. And he laid hold on the dragon, that serpent of old, who is the devil and Satan, and bound him for a thousand years. Revelation 20:1-2

These angels are also the ones that help us chain the spirits of sorcerers and witches that come in their astral bodies to attack the body of Christ, they are powerful enough to put them in chains and arrest the major powers and principalities.

Executing Angels

These are the angels who execute the judgments of God over cities and nations, bringing forth the Lord's justice over wickedness; the wine press of the Earth has been treaded many times.

And another angel came out of the Temple, which is in Heaven, he also having a sharp sickle. And another angel came out from the altar, who had power over fire, and cried with a loud cry to him that had the sharp sickle, saying, "Thrust in thy sharp sickle and gather the clusters of the vine of the earth, for her grapes are fully ripe."

Revelation 14:17-18

Angels to the Churches

These are the angels that help and minister the church in each city. These type of angels are very useful because they bring forth strategies from Heaven and reveal God's thoughts regarding the way He wants to build His Church.

The mystery of the seven stars which thou sawest in My right hand, and the seven golden candlesticks: the seven stars are the angels of the seven churches, and the seven candlesticks which thou sawest are the seven churches.

Revelation 1:20

SECTION III

THE BOOK OF REVELATION 'S
SECONDARY SUBJECTS

17 THE GREAT TRIBULATION

I n the previous section we saw how the people of *Israel* were living in a time of great tribulation, which culminated in God's great judgment upon *Jerusalem*. The temple was destroyed and the city set ablaze.

The Apostle John writes his prophetic message and lets them know God has not abandoned them but instead He is about to manifest His righteousness in an extraordinary manner.

He begins the *Book of Revelation* by letting them know that he himself is part of the tribulation.

*I, John, who also am your brother and companion **in the tribulation** and in the Kingdom and patience of Jesus Christ, was on the isle that is called Patmos, for the Word of God and for the testimony of Jesus Christ.*
Revelation 1:9

In the *Book of Revelation,* Chapter 7, he mentions a tribulation; due to its context it leads me to believe that he is referring to the Church of all times. If indeed the Early Church lived in a huge tribulation, we also need to overcome our own tribulations to serve God effectively.

This chapter talks about the manifestation of the Kingdom of God in the midst of our tribulations, whether personal or collectively.

Let's remember that we are studying the **Book of Revelation** as the living government of Christ with His saints.

> *And one of the elders answered, saying unto me, "Who are these that are arrayed in white robes, and from whence have they come?"*
> *And I said unto him, "Sir, thou knowest." And he said to me, "These are they that came out **of great tribulation**[26], and have washed their robes and made them white in the blood of the Lamb..."* Revelation 7:13-14

> **For this reason they are [now] before the [very] throne of God and serve Him day and night in His sanctuary (temple);** *and He Who is sitting upon the throne will protect and spread His tabernacle over and shelter them with His presence.*
> *They shall hunger no more, neither thirst any more; neither shall the sun smite them, nor any ascorching heat.*
> **For the Lamb Who is in the midst of the throne will be their Shepherd, and He will guide them to the springs of the waters of life;** *and God will wipe away every tear from their eyes.* Revelation 7:15-17 AMP

---

[26] Some manuscripts do not include the words "the great": *"these are they that came out of great tribulation." Douay Bible*

This passage has traditionally been interpreted as a future great tribulation, a sort of a third world war where millions of people die and are brought before the throne of God. First it is important to notice that these people "Come out of" great tribulation. This means they did not die but came out of it. So, from verse 15 on, we see a parallel to *The Book of Revelation*, Chapter 21, which **is the manifestation of God's tabernacle over the Earth** and the Kingdom of God established by the Messiah.

Be reminded that we studied the *basic themes* of interpretation, which shed light for us to interpret the secondary subjects, or the ones derived from these.

The fact that the Lamb shepherds those in white garments and leads them to fountains of water makes it clear to us that they are not in Heaven but on Earth where the spiritual waters of Christ are needed. In Heaven there are no dry places, and nobody needs to be led to the fountains of water – which are the life of Jesus. They are already eternally immersed in Him.

These points set the standard for our interpretation, since throughout the centuries God's tabernacle with men is the Church of Jesus Christ on Earth. God's tabernacle will not be established after a future world war; it has already been established in the midst of His people. We are the temple of God, and His throne is in the midst of His Church. We, therefore, serve Him continually.

The way I see this passage, John is talking about the victorious Church; those who overcome their own individual tribulations and live by the standards set by Jesus in the letters to the seven churches of Asia. It refers to those who have washed their clothes in the blood of the Lamb and serve God in the understanding of His throne and His Kingdom. They have become true kings and priests unto God ministering from His tabernacle where God's presence continually comes or **(erchomai)** to His people. The Spirit of God continually manifests himself as a cloud of glory in our midst, and Jesus is revealed to us from glory to glory. **We are continually being baptized in the Holy Spirit, which is the cloud that carries His presence.**

Throughout the centuries, in every tongue and nation, there is an invisible barrier that has to be crossed: these are the tribulations that bind us to this world until Jesus is formed in us; then we will rule and reign with Him. Those who allow themselves to be led by the Spirit are the ones who are before the throne aligned with what the Lord wants to say and do.

> *... strengthening the souls of the disciples, exhorting them to continue in the faith, and saying, "We must go through many **tribulations** enter the kingdom of God."*
>
> *Acts 14:22*

> *If **we endure** we shall also reign with Him.*
>
> *2 Timothy 2:12a*

When we endure suffering of any kind, it is for the purpose of the Kingdom of God to be manifest in our lives. As we understand this, something powerful forms within us.

The Kingdom of God and His throne begin to convey the answers to us and we see victory over that particular tribulation. This overcomming power emerges from within us, positioning us in a new level of authority and government over that area of our lives.

When we see victory over our tribulations, we are taken to the springs of life in Christ, and His tabernacle grows within us.

When I suffer, I learn to reign!

My little children, over whom I travail in birth again until Christ be formed in you... Galatians 4:19

As we talk about God's judgments in the course of this study, we will see that He has sent many tribulations of great devastation to humanity, which are applicable to Jesus' prophecies.

To think that the Lord needs to bring a devastating destruction over the Earth so His Kingdom would be established is not a thought that lines up with the mind of Christ.

Certanly there are strong shakings coming to the Earth because The Lord needs to judge evil and men's abominations that are now overwhelming the world. Earth cannot take the sin of humanity any longer, and is vomiting iniquity through natural disasters. Yet God will make us who fear Him come out triumphant from any tribulation.

18   The Beast

T To address this subject, we will necessarily enter into the realm of speculation. Today's prophets and apostles are searching for revelation on this topic, and some have found it. As a prophetess of God, this is what the Lord has revealed to me, and I am sure, that other revelations can converge with this one to attain a full meaning.

In a literal sense, "the Beast" in the *Book of Revelation,* Chapter 13, refers to the *Roman Empire.* I believe this is due to Daniel's interpretation of Nebuchadnezzar's dream. He saw an enormous image composed of four kingdoms whose feet represented *Rome.* (Daniel 2:34-35)

This image is the full composition of the *Babylonian* system, or "the great harlot" whose final defeat comes when Jesus overcomes it at the cross and then sends His judgment over *Rome.*

*And the stone that smote the image **became a great mountain and filled the whole earth..***
And in the days of these kings shall the God of Heaven set up a Kingdom which shall never be destroyed; and the

*Kingdom shall not be left to other people, but it shall break in pieces and consume **all these kingdoms, and it shall stand for ever.*** *Daniel 2:35b, 44*

We see clearly how the **Kingdom of Messiah** is the great **Mount Zion** that was established over the whole Earth. ALL THOSE KINGDOMS WERE DESTROYED by the Rock that is Jesus. *Rome* was literally burned down several times after God's judgment was decreed over it.

On the eve of July 19th, 64 A.D., a fire began in *Rome* that lasted 9 days. Ten of the fourteen districts disappeared, and along with them the temple of Jupiter. History attributes this catastrophe to Emperor Nero.[27]

Regardless, this was not the only time *Rome* was burnt down, "the beast received a mortal wound but survived", another great fire took place in 69 A.D. during the empire of Vitellius, and a third fire destroyed it in the year 80 A.D. under the government of Emperor Titus.[28]

Beasts in the Bible are symbols of empires controlled by dominions of darkness, *not of individuals.*

The ***Book of Revelation*** doesn't mention "an antichrist" but "a beast." John is the only apostle who uses the word "antichrist," and he does it in relation to a spirit that already was moving among them. He knew what he was talking about, since he is the one who received the ***Book of Revelation.***

---

[27] Wikipedia- Great Fire Of Rome.
[28] Ibid, Wikipedia- Great Fire Of Rome

However, every generation has to defeat the spirit of the antichrist.

*Little children, it is the last time: and as ye have heard that **antichrist** shall come, even now are there many antichrists; whereby we know that it is the last time.*

1 John 2:18

*Who is a liar but he that denieth that Jesus is the Christ? He is **antichrist** that denieth the Father and the Son.*

1 John 2:22

*For many deceivers are entered into the world, who confess not that Jesus Christ is come in the flesh. This is a deceiver and an **antichrist.*** 2 John 7

"The Beast" is the demonic spirit behind every *Babylonian* system throughout history. It's the spirit of humanism that gives rise to the ideology of a superman rising as God; it's the fallen man ruled by the *tree of good and evil;* it's Cain's homicidal seed that grows from generation to generation, promoting lawlessness on Earth and opposing the true God.

Beloved, believe not every spirit, but test the spirits whether they are of God, because many false prophets have gone out into the world. Hereby know ye the Spirit of God: Every spirit that confesseth that Jesus Christ is come in the flesh, is of God.
*And every spirit that confesseth not that Jesus Christ is come in the flesh, is not of God; and such is **the spirit of Antichrist,** whereof ye have heard that it should come,*

and **even now already it is in the world.**
Ye are of God, little children, and **have overcome them,**
because greater is He that is in you than he that is in the
world.
They are of the world; therefore they speak of the
world, and the world heareth them.

1 John 4:1-5

THE MARK OF THE BEAST

Whenever the Lord speaks about marking men in the Bible, in all the other cases it has always been a spiritual one.

Cain is marked to be protected when he was cursed to be a fugitive and vagabond in the world, and this mark was spiritual.

When we see the angels marking the chosen ones, they don't put a tatoo or a microchip in their forheads, but a seal of light that is visible in the spiritual realm.

The same thing happens when we talk about the "mark of the beast." This is visible as a seal of darkness that God and the demons can clearly see.

Being marked by the beast occurs when someone's mind (in the forehead) and actions (right hand) are controlled by the systems of this world in full corruption. Being marked is being totally sold out to darkness, unchanging, a lover of darkness more than light.

For men shall be lovers of their own selves, covetous,
boasters, proud, blasphemers, disobedient to parents,

unthankful, unholy, without natural affection, trucebreakers, false accusers, incontinent, fierce, despisers of those that are good, traitors, heady, highminded, lovers of pleasures more than lovers of God;

2 Timothy 3:2-4

*Now as Jannes and Jambres withstood Moses, so do these also resist the truth: **men of corrupt minds, reprobate concerning the faith.*** *2 Timothy 3:8*

The "right hand" also speaks about the authority and the power of our own will to make decisions.

My husband has a powerful revelation on the subject of "the mark of the beast." He saw Cain being marked because of his sin of murder. This mark is the mindset of the serpent, which is the beast in the *Garden of Eden,* who entered Cain as the result of the fall. This is not the mark God gave him to protect him, but the one satan implanted in his soul. This mark passed on as a seed through the generations, carrying the unrepentant attitude of Cain.

It is from Cain's seed that our entire commercial system developed, which that is under the control of the King of Tyrus, the god of trade and commerce, and under Mammon, the god of riches. Cain is the first person mentioned in the Bible to build a city, which was the first form of society. This was the first city satan ruled and then perfected as the ancient city of *Babylon.*

*And Cain knew his wife; and she conceived, and bare Enoch: **and he builded a city**, and called the name of the city, after the name of his son, Enoch.*

231

And unto Enoch was born Irad: and Irad begat Mehujael: and Mehujael begat Methusael: and Methusael begat Lamech.

And Lamech took unto him two wives: the name of the one was Adah, and the name of the other Zillah.

*And Adah bare Jabal: he was the father of such as dwell in tents, and of such **as have cattle.***

*And his brother's name was Jubal: he was the father of all such **as handle the harp and organ.***

*And Zillah, she also bare Tubalcain, an instructer of **every artificer in brass and iron:** and the sister of Tubalcain was Naamah.*   *Genesis 4:17-22*

Let's remember that the great *Babylon* is the city that rules over all the kings of the Earth, and that she controls the economical world system. When John is watching her judgment in Heaven, he tells about the merchants' great sorrow as they saw her burning in fire.

And the woman which thou sawest is that great city, which reigneth over the kings of the earth.

The merchants of these things, which were made rich by her, shall stand afar off for the fear of her torment, weeping and wailing,

And the voice of harpers, and musicians, and of pipers, and trumpeters, shall be heard no more at all in thee; and no craftsman, of whatsoever craft he be, shall be found any more in thee; and the sound of a millstone shall be heard no more at all in thee;

Revelation 17:18; 18:15, 22

There is a form of commerce that is righteous, based on the principles of God, which is a blessing to many, and differs totally from the evil one where *Babylon* controls people through greed and by abusing others to get gain.

Being marked by "The Beast" is having the mark of evil, the mark of Cain. These are the kinds of people Jude talks about in his epistle.

For there are certain men crept in unawares, who were before of old ordained to this condemnation, ungodly men, turning the grace of our God into lasciviousness, and denying the only Lord God, and our Lord Jesus Christ.

Jude 4

*Woe unto them! for they have gone in the **way of Cain,** and ran greedily after the error of Balaam for reward, and perished in the gainsaying of Core.*

These are spots in your feasts of charity, when they feast with you, feeding themselves without fear: clouds they are without water, carried about of winds; trees whose fruit withereth, without fruit, twice dead, plucked up by the roots;

Raging waves of the sea, foaming out their own shame; wandering stars, to whom is reserved the blackness of darkness for ever.

And Enoch also, the seventh from Adam, prophesied of these, saying, Behold, the Lord cometh with ten thousands of his saints,

To execute judgment upon all, and to convince all that are ungodly among them of all their ungodly deeds which they have ungodly committed, and of all their hard speeches which ungodly sinners have spoken against him.

These are murmurers, complainers, walking after their own lusts; and their mouth speaketh great swelling words, having men's persons in admiration because of advantage. Jude 11-16

Six is the number of man. The code of the beast is 666, which is the number of man that exalts himself over God, the superman who is his own god, who worships satan in all his disguised forms such as money, lust, and all kind of perversion.

Today we see this kind of thinking in the "new age" and in books such as *The Secret*. We see the abominable abuse of corrupted men contolling the stock market and the financial destiny of nations. Sexual depravation, greed, and crime are getting to intolerable climaxes.

The 666 is not a microchip, neither a credit card, nor a tatoo. It is the spiritual mark of the evil men who oppose God.

THE TIMES IN THE
BOOK OF REVELATION

THE TIMES IN THE *BOOK OF REVELATION*

F rom the beginning of our study, we saw how the dimensions of God are not limited by time in the Earth. The clocks of men do not run Heaven. God is Eternal, and there is no time in Him.

He is the One Who was, Who is, and Who comes or is continually coming (erchomai). He is the great "I Am," the eternal present Who manifests Himself within the temporality of man. For this reason, a heavenly book such as the *Book of Revelation* cannot be interpreted with times on Earth.

In Chapter 10, when John is about to eat the small book of prophecy, we see the angel tell him that time *ceased to be.*

And he swore by Him that liveth for ever and ever, who created heaven and the things that are therein, and the earth and the things that are therein, and the sea and the things which are therein, that **there should be time no longer,** *but that in the days of the voice of the seventh*

*angel, when he shall begin to sound, **the mystery of
God should be finished, as He hath declared to His
servants the prophets.***

Revelation 10:6-7

The mystery of God is consummated when Jesus takes the
Throne sitting at the right hand of the Majesty on High. From here
onward, His Kingdom has no end.

The true Church enters the Kingdom and into the timeless
dimension of God from where He governs. The little book the
angel gives John is the government manual for the prophetic
dimension of the Kingdom. If we understand this timeless nature
of Heaven, it makes it easy for us to interpret some of the passages
such as the *thousand years*.

1. THE THOUSAND YEARS OF THE BOOK OF REVELATION

*And I saw an angel come down from Heaven, having the
key to the bottomless pit and a great chain in his hand.
And he laid hold on the dragon, that serpent of old, who is
the devil and Satan, and bound him for a thousand years.
And he cast him into the bottomless pit, and shut him
up and set a seal upon him, that he should deceive the
nations no more till the thousand years should be fulfilled;
and after that he must be loosed a little season.*

Revelation 20:1-3

It's important to understand this expression, *the thousand years*
from its Hebrew word, which is **atid lavo.** This literally means "the

236

coming age" and is also used as a term that means "the Messianic age." In other words, as we enter the prophetic dimension, which is Messiah's Kingdom, we enter into the timelessness of His Kingdom.

"A thousand" as we previously saw, is the number that symbolyzes that which is perfect: 10x10x10 this is Heaven, God's spiritual Kingdom. "We will reign one thousand years" means we will rule from the spiritual world. The Kingdom of Christ on Earth is eternal; it doesn't end in a limited period of a thousand years.

*Of the increase of His government and peace there shall be no end, upon the throne of David and upon His Kingdom, to order it and to establish it with judgment and with justice from **henceforth even forever.** The zeal of the LORD of hosts will perform this.* Isaiah 9:7

We see this as well in the expression used by Peter:

But, beloved, be not ignorant of this one thing: that with the Lord one day is as a thousand years, and a thousand years as one day. 2 Peter 3:8

The fact that Peter makes the comparison between a day and a thousand years clearly makes us understand that it's not dealing with a precise time period. Among the Hebrews, the day of YHWH carries the understanding of "a coming future" or "the beginning of the Messianic age."[29]

---

[29] Same as footnote #23

2. SATAN BOUND AND THEN LOOSED

And when the thousand years are expired, Satan shall be loosed out of his prison, and shall go out to deceive the nations to the four quarters of the earth - Gog and Magog - to gather them together for battle, the number of whom is as the sand of the sea. Revelation 20:7-8

We clearly understand this passage when we learn to live in the dimensions of the Kingdom of God, when we genuinely stop being of this world and instead depend on a Kingdom whose laws and physics are very different from the Earthly ones. The devil has been bound for us; he can never penetrate the Kingdom of God to bring us harm.

Furthermore, to live in this spiritual reality is a continuous victory. The enemy has been thrown out of Heaven's access he once had and now lives among the nations of the Earth, deceiving them. It's outside the Kingdom where he is loose and where the battle is, and millions of people, Christians included, are living the devils' onslaught because of not having entered the dimensions of the Spirit of God.

Now, even though we have entered the Kingdom of God and live within the eternay of God (thousand years) it's by going through trials and tribulations that we mature in Christ. God allows satan to interfere in our lives for our own growth.

The expression "satan will be loosed to deceive the nations" has to do with these trials we have to overcome, even if we are kings and priests. He is loose for a short time in our daily walk to fulfill this purpose. Messiah's Kingdom is eternal; that's how it was prophesied to be. Nowhere in the Old Testament was it written that the reign of Messiah would be for a limited time of "a thousand years." In Jesus, Heaven and Earth are joined together, and this truth applies for both dimensions.

*And I will make her lame a remnant, and her that was cast far off a strong nation; and the LORD shall reign over them in Mount Zion **from hence forth, even for ever.***
Micah 4:7

*And He will reign over the house of Jacob **throughout the ages; and of His reign there will be no end.***
Luke 1:33

In Hebraic gematria[30] the expression "Gog and Magog" (*Gog and Magog*) form the number 70. The Jewish sages interpret this as the 70 gentile nations, which represent the world. Nevertheless, the Bible doesn't say that God is going to gather the nations for the battle but only Gog and Magog. We know this because in Greek, the pronoun "them" is in the masculine case as opposed to "nations," which is a neutral noun.

*And when the thousand years are expired, Satan shall be loosed out of his prison, and shall go out to deceive the nations to the four quarters of the earth - Gog and Magog - to gather **them** together for battle, the number of whom is as the sand of the sea.*
Revelation 20:7-8

---

[30] Among the Hebrews there is a science named Gematria through which every letter of the alphabet has a number and these in turn carry a symbolism worthy to interpret.

If we paraphrase this Bible passage, it would say something like this: "Outside the dimensions of God's Kingdom (1,000 years) the devil, out of his prison, carries on deceiving the nations, but God will combat these spirits."

CONCLUSION

Many are the themes found in the **Book of Revelation,** and it would take me several volumes to go into greater detail in each one. Some are quite profound and require us to first digest what I mention in this book. The **Kingdom of God** has no end; neither does its revelation or the **Book of Revelation** itself.

It is up to us to know Him in the revelation of His glory. It's our duty to discover how to govern with Him and discover our kingship territory. Therefore, this book has no end; it is only the first one God grants me to write, so… it shall CONTINUE.

BLESSING

*And he said unto me, These sayings are faithful and true: and the **Lord God of the holy prophets** sent his angel to shew unto his servants the things which must shortly be done.*

Behold, I come quickly: blessed is he that keepeth the sayings of the prophecy of this book. And, behold, I come quickly; and my reward is with me, to give every man according as his work shall be. I am Alpha and Omega, the beginning and the end, the first and the last. Blessed are they that do his commandments, that they may have right to the tree of life, and may enter in through the

240

gates into the city. For without are dogs, and sorcerers, and whoremongers, and murderers, and idolaters, and whosoever loveth and maketh a lie. I Jesus have sent mine angel to testify unto you these things in the churches. I am the root and the offspring of David, and the bright and morning star. And the Spirit and the bride say, Come. And let him that heareth say, Come. And let him that is athirst come. And whosoever will, let him take the water of life freely.

For I testify unto every man that heareth the words of the prophecy of this book, If any man shall add unto these things, God shall add unto him the plagues that are written in this book:

And if any man shall take away from the words of the book of this prophecy, God shall take away his part out of the book of life, and out of the holy city, and from the things which are written in this book.

He which testifieth these things saith, Surely I come quickly. Amen. Even so, come, Lord Jesus.

The grace of our Lord Jesus Christ be with you all. Amen.

Revelation 22: 6-7, 12-21

God is inviting you to be His wife, so as His Body we can overcome and govern jointly with Him. He has prepared a unique and precious revelation about Jesus Christ for you. This is the authority of your reigning and through it you call the lost world in to drink of Him, the true waters of life.

We are the temple of God, the city of the living God; our doors are continuously open so that anyone who washes their garments can enter in. The Lamb is our light, and we will reign with Him from age to age. If you are truly thirsty, come and drink of the waters of His Kingdom, and you will be satisfied.

Amen.

SECTION IV

THE FOLLOWING APPENDIXES - THAT I WILL CALL INSTRUMENTS- WILL HELP YOU REACH YOUR OWN CONCLUSIONS

T hese are the four main words theologically applied when one wants to study Christ's Second Coming.

When we referred to the power of preconceived ideas we found out how these influence our manner of interpreting Scripture. It was revealing to see how even dictionaries in English, Spanish, and other languages distort the meaning of the word *Apocalypse.* Now we find ourselves again with the same dilemma as we try to study these four words.

These are translated respectively as: *presence* **(parousia),** shining **(epiphaneia),** revelation **(apokalupsis),** *coming* **(erchomai** in the *aoristo* tense.) Christian dictionaries, however, add a parenthesis to each of their meanings: (applied to the Second Coming of Christi, This thought does not appear in a secular dictionary.

Therefore, when we try to find the definitions in this Scripture in our Christian dictionaries, we run into a phrase that compels us towards a certain direction: the *Second Coming* as a futuristic, unique fact. This eliminates the possibility of interpreting this other than the *Second Coming* of Christ in His resurrected body. However, there is a Coming where He is **already** in our midst, where the old system has been judged.

245

We have this *Second Coming* concept so preconceived in such full detail that if God wants to shed a different or greater light than the one taught by our traditions, this preconception represents a major obstacle.

Jesus will return; there is no discussion about that. My point is that not all of the Scriptures to which we apply the *Second Coming* refer to that alone.

Let's analyze these words with a teachable spirit and see what God may be trying to tell us which maybe we haven't yet seen in full clarity.

1. Parousia[31]: This word appears 24 times[32] in the New Testament, and in all of them it means "presence." Nouns are never conjugated – only verbs are. In most cases it refers to the presence of Christ that we can enjoy today.

Jesus has manifested His presence in many forms. During His First Coming He came in the flesh, and in the Old Testament He appeared as the Angel of the Lord. Since His ascension, we have had manifestations of His presence in different levels; from a heavy atmosphere charged with His Spirit, which becomes almost tangible, to totally visible appearances in which He can be seen.

---

[31] ***Strong Concordance 3952 parousia,*** from the present participle of 3918; a being near, i.e. advent (often, return; specially, of Christ to punish Jerusalem, or finally the wicked); (by implication) physically, aspect: — coming, presence.
3918. pareimi, from 3844 and 1510 (including its various forms); to be near, i.e. at hand; neuter present participle (singular) time being, or (plural) property: — come, x have, be here, + lack, (be here) present.

[32] Matthew 24:3, 27, 37 39. 1 Cor. 15:23, 16:15. 2 Cor. 7:6 and 7, 10:10, Phil. 1:26 2:12. 1 Thes. 2:19, 3:13, 4:15, 5:23. 2 Thes. 2:1, 2:8, 2:9. James 5:7, 8:2 Peter 1:16, 3:4, 3:12. 1 John 2:28.

Jesus has many forms in His glorified body, and His face transforms in many ways. He had the form of a gardener when He appeared to Mary at the tomb, and she did not recognize Him. He took a different form when He walked with His disciples on the road to Emaus, and they did not recognize Him either.

He would appear and disappear in their midst, and He would walk through walls. John saw Him in one form walking among the candlesticks and in another, dressed in blood riding a white horse. He saw Him as a Lamb and as a Lion.

This is important to know, because He is manifesting Himself in many ways to His Church, and each one is different.

In the flesh, Jesus was limited to a physical form, but in His glory His forms are infinite.

Let's see how this same word **parousia** is used, by the Apostle Paul referring to the "presence" of various people. Notice that when using this word, it does not refer to a sudden appearance of Jesus, but to a "presence" of the apostles among the church. (In the following verses, I changed the word coming used in the NKJ Bible, for the original word *presence* **(parousia)** so we can read the verse with the right word)

*I am glad of the presence **(parousia)** of Stephanas and Fortunatus and Achaicus: for that which was lacking on your part they have supplied.*   1 Corinthians 16:17

*Nevertheless God, that comforteth those that are cast down, comforted us by the presence **(parousia)** of Titus;*

247

*And not by his presence **(parousia)** only, but by the consolation wherewith he was comforted in you, when he told us your earnest desire, your mourning, your fervent mind toward me; so that I rejoiced the more.*
2 Corinthians 7:6-7

*For his letters, say they, are weighty and powerful; but his bodily presence **(parousia)** is weak, and his speech contemptible.*
2 Corinthians 10:10

*That your rejoicing may be more abundant in Jesus Christ for me by my presence **(parousia)** to you again.*
Philippians 1:26

*Wherefore, my beloved, as ye have always obeyed, not as in my presence **(parousia)** only, but now much more in my absence, work out your own salvation with fear and trembling.*
Philippians 2:12

As we study the Scriptures where we find the word **parousia** referring to Jesus' coming, we realize most of them can be applied to His presence in our midst, in the form of apparitions, sensing His intense presence in a meeting, or the manifestation of His judgments, especially those that came in the year 70 A.D.

Many wonderful things happen when we wait for the manifestation of His presence in our midst, which transforms us into His image when we see Him in His glory.

Now the Lord is that Spirit: and where the Spirit of the Lord is, there is liberty.
2 Corinthians 3:17

But we all, with open face beholding as in a glass the glory of the Lord, are changed into the same image from glory to glory, even as by the Spirit of the Lord.

2 Corinthians 3:17 -18

The Word of God also warns us to walk diligently because He comes to us suddenly to cleanse us so that an offering in righteousness can be given to Him.

Behold, I will send my messenger, and he shall prepare the way before me: and the Lord, whom ye seek, shall suddenly come to his temple, even the messenger of the covenant, whom ye delight in: behold, he shall come, saith the LORD of hosts.

But who may abide the day of his coming? and who shall stand when he appeareth? for he is like a refiner's fire, and like fullers' soap:

*And he shall sit as a refiner and purifier of silver: and he shall purify the sons of Levi, and purge them as gold and silver, that they may offer unto the LORD an offering **in righteousness.***

Then shall the offering of Judah and Jerusalem be pleasant unto the LORD, as in the days of old, and as in former years.

And I will come near to you to judgment; and I will be a swift witness against the sorcerers, and against the adulterers, and against false swearers, and against those that oppress the hireling in his wages, the widow, and the fatherless, and that turn aside the stranger from his right, and fear not me, saith the LORD of hosts.

Malachi 3:1-5

2. **Epiphaneia**[33]: This word refers to the *brightness of His glory and holiness*. This is the luminosity that manifests on His face when He acts in judgment or in deliverance. It is a synonym of the greek word **lampo** which means "to illuminate," and also of the word **diaphanes,** which means "a translucent shimmer, one we can see through."

This is the visible and glorious appearance of Christ, from a glow to a visible appearance; it's His shimmering holiness that exposes the sin in our hearts, and is the consuming fire that purifies and brings judgment.

This **epiphaneia** appearance is a manifestation full of light and glory.

Consequently, from now on we estimate and regard no one from a [purely] human point of view [in terms of natural standards of value]. [No] even though we once did estimate Christ from a human viewpoint and as a man, yet now [we have such knowledge of Him that] we know Him no longer [in terms of the flesh].
2 Corinthians 5:16 AMP

And then shall that wicked one be revealed, whom the Lord shall consume with the spirit of His mouth, and shall destroy with the brightness (epiphaneia) of His coming (parousia).
2 Thessalonians 2:8 Interlineal Greek Bible

---

[33] *Strong Concordance 2015. epiphaneia;* from 2016; a manifestation, i.e. (specially) the advent of Christ (past or future): — appearing, brightness.

To those who have waged high - level wars in the Spirit, this passage is very clear. In my book **High Level Warfare** I talk about what I have named *"God's spotlight."* Every war is a Judgment where God makes His Face blaze with a shining glow that brings all things to the light so they are judged. This same fire, which manifests itself when we fight, then turns towards us to purify us.

For they got not the land in possession by their own sword, neither did their own arm save them, but by Thy right hand and Thine arm and **the light of Thy countenance,** *because Thou hadst favor unto them.* Psalm 44:3

Turn us again, O LORD God of hosts; **cause Thy face to shine,** *and we shall be saved!.* Psalm 80:19

It's the epiphany of Jesus, the glow of His face that illuminates us and leads us into all spiritual truth.

For God, who commanded the light to shine out of darkness, hath shined in our hearts to give the light of the knowledge of the glory of God in the face of Jesus Christ.
2 Corinthians 4:6

To those who are intercessors, this manifest glowing, brilliant presence of Jesus happens quite often.

Those, who love His epiphany are the ones who sanctify themselves, and whom God trains in His righteousness to reign with Him. The crown of righteousness has been reserved for those who understand the judgments of His government.

Henceforth there is laid up for me a crown of righteousness which the Lord, the righteous Judge, shall give me on that Day -- and not to me only, but unto all those also who love His appearing. (diaphanes).　　　**2 Timothy 4:8**

3. Apokalupsis[34]: This word means "revelation, illumination, apparition" this is when either the Father or Jesus reveals something about Himself to the heart of man. In the **Book of Revelation**, which is the revelation of Jesus, we are immersed in His prophetic realm to see and understand His Heavenly character and how He acts; it's when He goes in and takes out from His secret treasures and brings them out to the light for us. It's also the revelation of the sentences of all His judgments

And Jesus answered and said unto him, "Blessed art thou, Simon Bar-Jonah, for flesh and blood hath not revealed ***(apokalupsis)*** *it unto thee, but My Father who is in Heaven."*　　　**Matthew 16:17**

It's the revelation of the knowledge of God that will fill the Earth as the waters cover the sea. It's in the revelation of our Messiah that we find all the treasures of God.

... that their hearts might be comforted, being knit together in love unto all the riches of the full assurance of understanding, that they may acknowledge the mystery of God, and of the Father, and of Christ, in whom are hid all the treasures of wisdom and knowledge.　　　**Colossians 2:2-3**

---

[34] **Strongs Concordance 602. apokalupsis,;** from 601; disclosure: — appearing, coming, lighten, manifestation, be revealed, revelation.

4. Erchomai: This is the word we encounter when Scripture talks about Jesus coming in the clouds. To realize what this means, we must understand what "clouds" mean to God. This theme was dealt with when we analyzed the clouds.

The key word here is *coming or come*, **erchomai** in the Greek *aoristo* tense. As I mentioned earlier in this book, this tense that does not exist in Spanish or English.

Let's look at a definition of this tense as expressed by a language professor, Justo Fernando Lopez:

"The *aoristo* expresses a duration that carries no interest for the speaker; it is sometimes of such a brief duration that it is reduced to a point (momentary aspect). The Greek term *aoristo* means 'indefinite, unlimited, without time limit.' Origin-wise, it was something such as the 'no-time', the verb without a direct temporal translation, something like eternity, or 'forever and ever.'

The *aoristo* denotes an action as occurring in the past without any reference to its progression, without expressing a completed action. The *aoristo* simply presents the action without any reference to its duration. The *aoristo* doesn't express duration or termination; it is therefore indeterminate, undefined."[35]

The ***aoristo*** is definitely not in a future tense. Jesus was specifically prophesying in this passage that He would come to

---

[35] Translated from Spanish. Hispanoteca, lengua y cultura, foro de cultura
http://www.hispanoteca.eu/Foro-preguntas/ARCHIVO-Foro/Indefinido%20y%20aoristo.htm

spiritually and eternally remain in the midst of His people.

5. Additional Words: Other words, used in certain verses, are also related to the *coming* of the Lord, and are interesting to study:

Phaneroo,[36] This word means to render apparent or make manifest, not necessarily a visible presence, but a perception. "When He shall appear (become apparent), we shall be like Him" (I Jn. 3:2).

The word *come,* in Revelation 2:25 has been translated from three different words according to the some of the greek dictionaries.

Age[37], means to lead, or an imperative of to come, "come on". **Akouoo**[38], means to give audience or to come to the ears.

The word *coming* in Revelation 1:7 also has been translated from different words.

Heko[39] This word stresses the point of arrival at a certain place,

---

[36] Nas Greek *5319. fanero/w phaneroo;* from 5318; to make visible, make clear: — appear (1), appeared (6), appears (3), become visible (1), becomes visible (1), disclose (1), disclosed (1), displayed (1), made evident (2), made known (1), made manifest (2), make clear (1), manifested (18), manifests (1), **revealed** (7), show (1), shown (1).

[37] *Strong Concordance 33. age,*; imperative of 71; properly, lead, i.e. **come** on: — go to 71. **ago,;** a primary verb; properly, to lead; by implication, to bring, drive, (reflexively) go, (specially) pass (time), or (figuratively) induce: — be, bring (forth), carry, (let) go, keep, lead away, be open.

[38] Greek Keys191. **ajkou/w** akouoœ; a primary verb; to hear (in various senses): — give (in the) audience (of), **come** (to the ears), (shall) hear(-er, -ken), be noised, be reported, understand.

[39] *Strong Concordance 2240. heko;* a primary verb; to arrive, i.e. be present (literally or figuratively): — come.

as I have come and I am here. "Hold fast till I COME (to you)."

Hikanos[40], means competent, as coming in a season. And **Erchomai.** (we already dealt with this one)

---

[40] **hikanos, from hiko (hikano or hikneomai,** akin to 2240) (to arrive); competent (as if coming in season), i.e. ample (in amount) or fit (in character): — able, + content, enough, good, great, large, long (while), many, meet, much, security, sore, sufficient, worthy.

INSTRUMENT 2
THE TIMES IN WHICH
THE EARLY CHURCH LIVED

S ince ancient times *Jerusalem* was the city that killed the prophets. The crowning of their guilt came when they killed the Son of God. This crime, the greatest one of all humanity, would usher in the great judgment of the wrath of God over the *City of David*. In the first century, The *Roman Empire*, joined to the Jewish leaders of that time, brought upon the budding Church great persecution and death. This continued during the reigns of ten Roman Emperors, in which Christians were thrown to the lions; crucified and burnt. Converting to Jesus implied a sure death and great tribulation. Day to day, the new believers buried their loved ones by the dozen.

Also during this time there were great revolts in which the Jews were trying to overthrow the Romans, that peaked to an unprecedented war that began in the year 66 A.D. and climaxed with the destruction of Jerusalem three and a half years later in the year 70 A.D.[41]

---

[41] Flavio Josepho. Jewish historian. His most important works were *The Jewish War* (c. 75) *and Antiquities of the Jews* (c. 94).[4] The Jewish War recounts the Jewish revolt against Roman occupation (66–70). http://en.wikipedia.org/wiki/Josephus

Jesus told his disciples about these approaching difficult times but He encouraged them by telling them He would end that tribulation by bringing forth the manifestation of His righteousness. The generation that was to crucify Him would assuredly be in lamentation.

From the end of Matthew, Chapter 23 we see Jesus talking about how the guilt of the fathers had reached its limit; this would happen when Jehovah would avenge the shed blood in *Jerusalem,* from Abel to Zechariah, son of Barachiah. This last prophet marked the period that was to be judged thereby putting an end to the ancient era.

We need to remember that Jesus' ministry on Earth was exclusivly to the Jews. God had judged Israel many times during its history, punishing them for their sins. This particular judgement was over the generation that openly rejected the Messiah in His coming in flesh, and cryed out for His crucifiction.

Jesus made lamentation for the earthly *Jerusalem,* the one He lived in and He announced its desolation in Matthew 23:32-39. In Chapter 24 He explained how this destruction would happen.

The main theme in this passage is the destruction of the temple and the whole ancient system in order to give way to the new. Jesus does not have to judge the earthly *Jerusalem* again with such devastation; this already happened. If we ignore history and only study the 24th chapter with a preconceived mentality of the "end of the world" happening in the future, in my opinion we will be making a serious mistake.

a) The Siege And Destruction Of Jerusalem In History

"We learn about the details of this uprising through the writings of Flavius Josephus, a Jewish military chief who, after surrendering to the Romans in 67A.D. became a part of General Titus entourage, assisting in the development of the expeditions from the Roman ranks. This is therefore a testimony of exception, of somebody who lived the conflict between the two sides.

The first Jewish-Roman War, also known as The Great Revolt, was the first of the three main rebellions of the Jews of the Judean province against the *Roman Empire* (Jewish-Romans wars) and took place in the years 66 and 73 A.D. It began in the year 66 A.D. initially because of Greek and Jewish religious tensions. It ended when Roman legions under Titus besieged and destroyed *Jerusalem,* set the temple on fire in the year 70 A.D. (three and a half years of conflict), demolished the main Jewish fortresses (especially *Massadah* in the year 73A.D.) and either enslaved or massacred a great portion of the Jewish population. (From 66 to 73A.D. makes seven years of conflict.)

Detail of the Arch of Titus depicting the stolen treasures from the *temple of Jerusalem*

(The seven-branch menorah, the golden table of the shewbread, the scrolls of the Law, and the veil from the Sancta Sanctorum.3)

b) The Siege on *Jerusalem*

The siege of *Jerusalem* was tougher than what Titus expected. Upon not being able to break the city's defenses in one single assault, the Roman army besieged it, establishing a permanent camp just outside the city. Fenced-in, *Jerusalem* lacked sufficient water and food for all those under siege, including thousand of pilgrims had recently arrived to celebrate the Jewish Passover. Now the Romans forcefully prevented them from leaving the city, exerting an even greater pressure on their already diminishing supplies. Inside *Jerusalem*, the people were dying by the thousands because of sickness and famine. However, the Jewish revolutionaries were not willing to surrender, and they hurled over the wall those pacifists who appeared suspicious.

The burning and destruction of Jerusalem by the Romans under the command of Emperor Titus.

Canvas by David Roberts 1850.

These are excavations of the location of the 2nd Temple of Jerusalem, destroyed by the Roman Army.

Photo provided by The Davidson Center.

In the summer of 70A.D., after demolishing the walls of *Jerusalem*, the Romans entered and looted the city. They attacked the *Antonia* fortress and soon after occupied the temple, which was set ablaze, and destroyed on the 9th of the Jewish month of Av. The citadel of Herodes fell the following month.

After King David, the first Jewish king who reigned over *Jerusalem* until its destruction by Titus 1039 went by. From its founding to its final destruction, 2077 years. Despite everything, its antiquity, riches, fame throughout the Earth, the great glory of its religion was of no value to prevent its destruction and demise. The Romans demolished the city walls in such a manner, and leveled them off in such a way, that who ever came by could barely believe it had ever been inhabited. " [31]

---

[31] Wikipedia http://en.wikipedia.org/wiki/Siege_of_Jerusalem_(70)

INSTRUMENT 3

THE SIGNS OF THE END

T his was the topic that Jesus spoke about to His disciples, showing them the signs they were to wait for. In Matthew 24 *(and analogous passages in Mark and Luke)* we see what was going to happen from the Earth's point of view, and in the *Book of Revelation* Jesus shows John how these events would be seen from Heaven. It then becomes important to analyze these facts from these two points of view to understand what Jesus wanted to say.

ANALYSIS OF MATTHEW 24 FROM THE ORIGINAL INTERLINEAL GREEK TEXTUAL BIBLE

The main theme in this passage is the destruction of the temple and the whole ancient system, to make way for the new." Matthew 24 contains various themes worthy to analyze in depth, which we have already touched upon in previous chapters. Therefore, we will now see it in its generic form:

*And Jesus went out and departed from the temple, and His disciples came to Him to show Him **the buildings of*** *the temple. And Jesus said unto them, "See ye not all these things? Verily I say unto you, there shall **not be left here one stone upon another that shall not be thrown down."** And as He sat upon the Mount of Olives, the disciples came unto Him privately, saying, "Tell us, when shall these things be? **And what shall be the sign of Thy presence (parousia[42]) and of the end of the age[43] (aion)? "*.* Mathew 24:1-3

Wanting to know when that *era* (aion) was going to end, the disciples asked Him that question. The Presence of Jesus here is not about the *Second Coming* of Christ as the Church has conceived it, but the manifestation of His righteousness. Jesus had to judge the *Jerusalem* of His days for the death of all the prophets and the sheer wickedness established in that religious system. He did not appear in the flesh, but His presence was manifested as a judgment. God wants us to open our spirits to understand how He prophesied in different ways aboout how He would manifest His coming after His ascension, which we have analyzed in depth previously.

He then speaks to them on how that moment would come about when God would act in His wrath, devastating the city. Upon God judging the former age, the Kingdom of God would be manifested and remain established.

---

[43] *Strong Concordance 3952. parousi÷a parousia, par-oo-see'-ah;* from the present participle of 3918; a being near, i.e. advent (often, return; specially, of Christ to punish Jerusalem, or finally the wicked); (by implication) physically, aspect: — coming, presence.

[44] *Strong Concordance 165. aijw÷n aion,* from the same as 104; properly, **an age;** by extension, perpetuity (also past); by implication, the world; specially (Jewish) a Messianic period (present or future): — age, course, eternal, (for) ever(-more), (n-)ever, (beginning of the while the) world (began, without **end**). Compare 5550.

And Jesus answered and said unto them, "Take heed that no man deceive you; for many shall come in My name, saying, 'I am Christ,' and shall deceive many. And ye shall hear of wars and rumors of wars. See that ye be not troubled, for all these things must come to pass, but the end is not yet. For nation shall rise against nation and kingdom against kingdom, and there shall be famines and pestilences and earthquakes in divers places.
All these are the beginning of sorrows.
Then **shall they deliver you up to be afflicted and shall kill you,** *and ye shall be hated by all nations for My name's sake..."* Matthew 24:4-9

Since the time of the Acts of the Apostles, Christians were persecuted and killed as I previously mentioned. Added to this were the internal wars between Jews who came from diverse parts of the land. John himself mentions this tribulation in the year 64 A.D. when he writes the *Book of Revelation.*[44]

I, John, who also am your brother and companion in the **tribulation and in the Kingdom and in the patience of Jesus Christ,** *was on the isle that is called Patmos, for the Word of God and for the testimony of Jesus Christ.*
Revelation 1:9

After the resurrection, Jesus took up the throne and sat as Lord of lords; however, the Father establishes a time mentioned in the

---

[44] Some think the *Book of Revelation* was written in the year 95A.D., but this theory fails on its own because the city of Jerusalem with the temple was destroyed in the year 70A.D. and Chaper 11:13 predicts its destruction. More accurate theories place it between 64 and 67 A.D. which is much more logical due to the content of the book.

Bible *as the time of His patience or the time of the patience of Jesus Christ,* in which He gives all the Jewish people an opportunity for salvation before releasing His judgment over the old Jerusalem.

> *And then shall many lose faith and shall betray one another and shall hate one another. And many false prophets shall rise and shall deceive many. And because iniquity shall abound, the love of many shall wax cold. But he that shall endure unto the end,*[45] ***(Greek: telos, appointed time),*** *same shall be saved. And this Gospel of the Kingdom shall be preached in all the inhabited land (all the world) for a witness unto all nations, and then shall* **the end of the age** *come.*   Matthew 24:10-14

We have two interesting groups of words to analyze here: *All the inhabited land and all the world.* In the original Greek we find the words *eis*[46] and *"oikoumene"*[47], which mean "a territory or a portion of the globe." It was also used to determine the territory of Roman Empire. This is why Paul addresses the Romans in this fashion:

> *But I ask, have they not heard? Yes, verily: "Their sound went out into all the earth, and their words* **unto the ends of the world."**   Romans 10:18

---

[45] *Strong Concordance 5056. telos* from a primary **tello** (to set out for a definite point or goal); properly, the point aimed at as a limit, i.e. (by implication) the conclusion of an act or state (termination (literally, figuratively or indefinitely), result (immediate, ultimate or prophetic), purpose); specially, an impost or levy (as paid): — + continual, custom, end(-ing), finally, uttermost. Compare 5411

[46] *Strong Concordance 1519. eis ice;* a primary preposition; to or into

[47] *Strong Concordance 3625. oikoumene;* feminine participle present passive of 3611 (as noun, by implication, of 1093); land, i.e. the (terrene part of the) globe; specially, *the Roman Empire:* — earth, world.

*... which has come unto you, as it has **in all the world,** and bringeth forth fruit, as it doth also in you since the day ye heard of it and knew the grace of God in truth.*

Colossians 1:6

Jesus here is not talking in the context of the *preaching of the Gospel to all the Earth,* He was referring to the territory to where judgment was coming, which was the *Roman Empire* and the Old Covenant.

When ye therefore shall see the abomination of desolation, spoken of by Daniel the prophet, standing in the holy place (whosoever readeth, let him understand)...

Matthew 24:15

Jesus calls us to understand something about this verse in Matthew that the *abomination of desolation* was not just an isolated event that was soon going happen, but it was something that had happened, and would repeatedly happen.

When Daniel interpreted Nebuchadnezzar's dream, he saw a great statute formed by four empires: *the Babylonian, Mede-Persian, Greek,* and *Roman.* In another vision he again saw these same kingdoms represented by four beasts that came and conquered Israel.

The *abomination of desolation* occurs in three of these empires:

1. Babylon: After the Prophet Ezekiel was taken captive during the Babylonian Captivity, he saw in a vision the temple defiled with Babylonian gods. He saw the statue of Tammuz in the

265

Holy Place, and abominations written on the walls of the temple (Ezekiel 8).

2. Greece: In the year 164 B.C. Antiochus IV Epiphanes, a king in the Seleucid dynasty - one of the four kingdoms into which the Greek Empire was divided - desecrated the temple in *Jerusalem*. His name means "god manifested." He ordered a statue of Zeus to be placed in the Holy of Holies, and abominable things, such as a pig, to be sacrificed upon the altar.

3. Rome: In the year 70 A.D. pagan soldiers penetrated the temple and the Holy of Holies, destroying the ritual items and holy utensils. In their place they put up the emperor's symbols and standards. Some theologians allude to the idea that the *abomination of desolation* was fulfilled at that moment since, according to Jewish Law, nothing impure could penetrate the temple, much less the Holy of Holies.

We see through these events how *the abomination of desolation* took place on several occasions when ungodly people profaned the temple. In my opinion, Jesus was not only talking about one single act, but about a repetitive pattern, which ended with the destruction of *Jerusalem*.

In Daniel's interpretation of the statue in Nebuchadnezzar dream, Jesus is the Rock coming out of the sky, which destroys the statue by striking its iron and clay feet, which represent the *Roman Empire*.

Thou sawest until a stone was cut out without hands, which smote the image upon his feet that were of iron *and clay, and broke them to pieces. Then were the iron, the clay, the brass, the silver, and the gold broken to pieces together, and became like the chaff of the summer threshing floors; and the wind carried them away, that no place was found for them. **And the stone that smote the image became a great mountain and filled the whole earth.*** Daniel 2:34-35

John, in the **Book of Revelation,** sees the heavenly fulfillment of that moment when he describes the fall of the great *Babylon,* which is the compendium of those four empires. Jesus is the Rock that came out from Heaven, bringing the authority of His Kingdom to destroy the system of the world.

Then a mighty angel took up a stone like a great millstone and threw it into the sea, saying, "Thus with violence the great city Babylon shall be thrown down, and shall not be found anymore. Revelation 18:21

Mount Zion is the government of God that fills the whole Earth with His Righteousness. This is the *mountain* above all mountains and *the Kingdom* above all kingdoms.

The *Mountain of the Lord* is already all over the planet. This happened with the destruction of the *Roman Empire.* This why it is written that we have approached *Mount Zion,* not the physical mountain in Israel, but the one that fills the Earth.

But ye are come unto mount Zion, and unto the city of the living God, the heavenly Jerusalem, and to an innumerable company of angels. Hebrews 12:22

Now lets go back to our study of **Matthew 24** where Jesus is going to warn his disciples about the time of their escape from *Jerusalem*.

a) The Escape

It is historically known that during the first century the Church fled to the mountains to save their lives by heeding Jesus' warning about when *Jerusalem* would be conquered.

> *...then let them that be in Judea flee unto the mountains. Let him that is on the housetop not come down to take anything out of his house; neither let him that is in the field return back to take his clothes. And woe unto them that are with child, and to them that give suck in those days! But pray ye that your flight be not in the winter, neither on **the Sabbath day.**   Matthew 24:16-20*

The fact that He alluded to the *day of rest* clearly shows us He was referring to the Jews of His time period and not to the Church composed of Jews and Gentiles. For the Church, Jesus is our *day of rest*.

> *For if Joshua had given them rest, then He would not afterward have spoken of another day.*
> *There remains therefore a rest for the people of God.*
> *For he who has entered His rest has himself also ceased from his works as God did from His.*
> *Hebrews 4:8-10*

> *Let no man therefore judge you in meat or drink, or in*

*respect to a holy day or the new moon or the Sabbath days, **which are a shadow of things to come,** but the body is of Christ.*   *Colossians 2:16-17*

We cannot place this *'escape'* 21 centuries into the future, as the non-Jewish Church does not celebrate the Sabbath, neither is this part of the New Testament doctrine preached by the Apostles to the gentiles.[48] When Jesus was carrying the Cross He spoke to the women who were weeping for Him about the difficult times that were at hand.

But Jesus, turning unto them, said, "Daughters of Jerusalem, weep not for Me, but weep for yourselves and for your children. For behold, the days are coming in which they shall say,   "Blessed are the barren, and the wombs that never bore and the breasts which never gave suck."   *Luke 23:28-29*

He was not referring to women thousands of years later, but to those who were weeping at that moment, because He knew of the impending destruction and how difficult it would be for them to flee under those conditions.

Jesus was referring to a time of tribulation that would take place in the 37 years between His resurrection and the fall of *Jerusalem.* These were the wars among the Jews and the persecution of

---

[48] Today the Messianic Jews continue to celebrate the Sabath along with a number of churches that want to identify with the Jewish practices. But this is not a general rule, neither is found in the New Testament an apostolic ordenance where Christians should observe the Judaic Law.

Christians.[49] Further on I will talk about the great tribulation from the heavenly point of view in the **Book of Revelation.**

For then shall be great tribulation, such as was not since the beginning of the world to this time, no, nor ever shall be.   Matthew 24:21

Jesus was referring to that period of time between His resurrection and the fall of Jerusalem. This period is historically known as the war of the Jews and also as the time of Christian persecutions in the first century.

And unless those days should be shortened, there should no flesh be saved; but for the elect's sake, those days shall be shortened.
Then if any man shall say unto you, "Lo, here is Christ," or "there," believe it not.
For there shall arise false chrisms and false prophets and shall show great signs and wonders, insomuch that, if it were possible, they shall deceive the very elect.
Behold, I have told you before.
Therefore, if they shall say unto you, `Behold, He is in the desert!' go not forth; or `Behold, He is in the secret chambers!' believe it not.
For as the lightning cometh out of the east and shineth even unto the west, so shall also the presence (Parousia) of the Son of Man be.   Matthew 24:22-27

---

[49] Therefore I judge that we should not trouble those from among the Gentiles who are turning to God, but that we write to them to abstain from things polluted by idols, from sexual immorality, from things strangled, and from blood.
For Moses has had throughout many generations those who preach him in every city, being read in the synagogues every Sabbath."   Acts 15:19-21

This word **parousia** in verse 27 is the same as in verse 24:3 where Jesus is talking about the manifestation of His righteousness, not about a physical appearance.

The comparison Jesus intends to make is not the rushing speed of a thunderbolt, but to its light that illuminates the whole sky in the midst of the darkness produced by a storm. He is talking about the influence of His presence **(parousia)** bringing illumination to the conscience as the lightning lights up the whole sky.

Jesus is explaining that the manifested righteousness of His presence (parousia) was not something private or hidden, but something that was to be obviously recognized by *Israel*. He was not going to be like the false Christs who hide in the desert and in their secret chambers, but His light would greatly influence and shine over all humanity, and His judgments visible to every eye.

A parallel verse in the Textual Bible says:

*For as the lightning that lighteneth from one extreme to the other in heaven and **where the Heavens join with the Earth, so shall also the Son of Man be in His day.***
Luke 17:24

This verse affirms what Paul says about the union of Heaven and Earth in Jesus (Ephesians 1:9). This is the living essence of the Kingdom that opens up for us the heavenly dimensions within Him.

For wheresoever the carcass is, there will the eagles be gathered together.
Matthew 24:28

In my opinion this refers to the great slaughter that was to come. The Jews who were left in Israel who did not convert to Christ *(thus they were dead in their spirit)* took refuge at the fortress of *Massadah* where they committed mass suicide in 73 A.D.[50]

Immediately after the tribulation of those days shall the sun be darkened and the moon shall not give her light, and the stars shall fall from heaven and the powers of the heavens shall be shaken,   Matthew 24:29

This passage is parallel to the one in 2 Peter 3:9-10 that we previously studied, where the powers of darkness and the structures of this world were judged to make way for the new era of the government of Christ.

b) Jesus Comes In The Clouds

... and then shall appear the sign of the Son of Man in heaven. And then shall all the tribes of the earth[51] **(the Greek word ge),** *mourn, and they shall see the Son of Man coming[52] (erchomai) in the clouds of heaven with power and with great glory.*   Matthew 24:30

---

[50] The rampart was complete in the spring of 73, after probably two to three months of siege, allowing the Romans to finally breach the wall of the fortress with a battering ram on April 16.[3] According to Josephus, when Roman troops entered the fortress, they discovered that its 960 inhabitants had set all the buildings but the food storerooms ablaze and committed a mass suicide.
http://en.wikipedia.org/wiki/Masada

[51] *Strong's Concordance 1093. ge;* contracted from a primary word; soil; by extension a region, or the solid part or the whole of the terrene globe (including the occupants in each application): — country, earth(-ly), ground, land, world.

[52] *Strong's Concordance 2064. erchomai,* er'-khom-ahee; middle voice of a primary verb **(used only in the present and imperfect tenses,** the others being supplied by a kindred (middle voice)

Let's be reminded that at the beginning of this chapter, Jesus unites *the sign of His coming with the end of the age.*

We will now analyze the word *coming* since we already analyzed the word *cloud* in Chapter 13.

The Greek word for coming is key here (**erchomai** in the *aoristo* tense).

Here again, *aoristo* is definitely not a word of the future tense. Jesus was specifically prophesying in this passage that He was to come to stay spiritually and eternally amidst His people. In other words, this Scripture is talking about a manifestation of Christ where He makes His glory and great power radiate limitlessly from eternity with the purpose to judge the iniquity that would bring an end to that age.

As of that moment, Jesus is endlessly and throughout the ages manifesting Himself in the life of His Church and making His enemies as His footstool.

For where two or three are gathered together in My name, there am I in the midst of them. "   *Matthew 18:20*

This passage from Matthew is related to Revelation 1:7 and Zechariah 12:10

Behold, He cometh (erchomai) with clouds, and every eye shall see Him, and they also who pierced Him; and all kindreds of the earth shall wail because of Him. Even so. Amen.   *Revelation 1:7*

273

The angel of the Lord was announcing to His people through John that Jesus was about to manifest His glory, coming to judge those who had pierced Him and those who were murdering the brethren. This was news of great joy for the Church living in Great Tribulation.

Jesus was quoting the passage prophesied by **Zechariah:**

*And I will pour upon the house of David and upon the inhabitants of Jerusalem the spirit of grace and of supplication; **and they shall look upon Me whom they have pierced,** and they shall mourn for Him as one mourneth for his only son, and shall be in bitterness for Him as one who is in bitterness for his firstborn. .*
Zechariah 12:10

This whole passage of Zechariah talks about the ensuing lamentation to occur when *Jerusalem* was to be destroyed in the year 70 A.D. Jesus was not talking about innocent Jews 21 centuries afterwards; He was referring to those who literally pierced Him.

In a spiritual sense, this also applies to us when we experience His *erchomai,* that breathtaking moment when eternity is manifested in our lives. When Christ comes to us and reveals to our hearts His suffering at the cross, the Holy Spirit convicts us of sin and we grieve for Him upon realizing that we ourselves have pierced Him by our iniquities.

c) The Clouds

I dedicated to This topic, which is of radical importance was discused in Chapter 13. For now, let's stay with the analysis of Matthew 24 that Jesus is talking about a manifestation of His presence that would bring an end to the temple in *Jerusalem* and to the ancient era. In the same manner that Jehovah manifested Himself as a pillar of cloud and fire, now He would manifest Himself as Jesus to judge the *Babylonian* system that had corrupted the priestly order of the Old Testament.

I want to make clear, that I am NOT saying that there will not be a physical manifestation of His Second Coming. I am saying that this particular Scripture refers to a spiritual manifestation of His presence.

And He shall send His angels with a great sound of a trumpet, and they shall gather together His elect from the four winds, from one end of heaven to the other.
"Now learn a parable of the fig tree: When his branch is yet tender and putteth forth leaves, ye know that summer is nigh.
So likewise ye, when ye shall see all these things, know that it is near, even at the doors.
Verily I say unto you, this generation shall not pass till all these things be fulfilled.
Heaven and earth shall pass away, but My Words shall not pass away.   *Mathew 24:31-35*

Jesus was speaking to *that* generation, who would experience a horrendous persecution, not to a generation 2000 years later. That generation was to suffer the intense persecution and killing of the first Christians, the many conflicts among the Jews, the intense war that started in the year 66A.D. and the siege of *Jerusalem.* Biblically speaking, a generation encompasses 40 years. He was talking to them. He was preparing them for what they were about to undergo. He placed a sense of urgency on them, which we repeatedly read in the first three chapters of the *Book of Revelation: "things which must shortly come to pass, I come quickly, "I stand at the door and knock."*

But of that day and hour, knoweth no man, no, not the angels of Heaven, but My Father only.
But as the days of Noah were, so shall also the coming of the Son of Man be.
For as in the days that were before the flood they were eating and drinking, marrying and giving in marriage, until the day that Noah entered into the ark and knew not until the flood came and took them all away, so shall also the coming **(parousia)** *of the Son of Man be.*
Matthew 24:36-39

These verses speak to us about the lack of reverence and unbelief from the people towards the words of their Messiah. Just as Noah went unheeded and everyone did as they pleased, likewise many of the Jewish people did not responded to the words of Jesus.

Then shall two be in the field; the one shall be taken and the other left.
Two women shall be grinding at the mill; the one shall be taken and the other left.   *Matthew 24:40-41*

Jesus was quoting Zechariah's prophecy and how one out of two were going to be taken captive.

For I will gather all nations against Jerusalem to battle; and the city shall be taken, and the houses rifled, and the women ravished. And half of the city shall go forth into captivity, and the residue of the people shall not be cut off from the city **where half of the citizens shall be taken captive and the rest will not.** *Zechariah 14:2*

Every prophecy about Jesus is coherent and must be confirmed according to the Old Testament, because it was He, Himself who prophesied about Himself through the prophets.

*Of this salvation the prophets have inquired and searched carefully, who prophesied of the grace that would come to you, searching what, or what manner of time, **the Spirit of Christ who was in them** was indicating when He testified beforehand the sufferings of Christ and the glories that would follow.* *1 Peter 1:10-11*

There is no passage in the Old Testament where Messiah is seen snatching up anybody from the planet. So this Scripture of Matthew can not be interpreted as people being raptured. I consider it is necessary to encourage you to take into account He who prophesied all things, Who is Christ, to reach a truthful conclusion of what He spoke to us.

"Watch therefore, for ye know not what hour your Lord doth come. (erchomai) *Matthew 24:42*

The verb is conjugated in *aoristo,* indicating to us again the surprising and eternal presence of the Lord when he would come.

But know this, that if the master of the house had known what hour the thief would come, he would have watched and not allowed his house to be broken into.

Therefore you also be ready, for the Son of Man is coming at an hour you do not expect.

"Who then is a faithful and wise servant, whom his master made ruler over his household, to give them food in due season?

Blessed is that servant whom his master, when he comes, will find so doing.

Assuredly, I say to you that he will make him ruler over all his goods.

But if that evil servant says in his heart, "My master is delaying his coming,'

and begins to beat his fellow servants, and to eat and drink with the drunkards,

the master of that servant will come on a day when he is not looking for him and at an hour that he is not aware of,

and will cut him in two and appoint him his portion with the hypocrites. There shall be weeping and gnashing of teeth.   *Matthew 24:43-51*

Jesus finishes his discourse by urging them to persevere in their faithfullness.

These verses were an encouragement to the early believers; they are also alive for us as a fundamental principle of our spiritual life. Jesus will always come to us manifesting His presence in our hearts, either through His glorious apparitions or in His *second Coming* in a physical body.

I will not leave you orphans; I will come to you. "A little while longer and the world will see Me no more, but you will see Me. Because I live, you will live also. **At that day you will know that I am in My Father, and you in Me, and I in you.**   John 14:18-20

Teaching them to observe everything that I have commanded you, and behold, I am with you aall the days (bperpetually, uniformly, and on every occasion), to the [very] close and consummation of the age. Amen (so let it be).   Matthew 28:28 AMP

When Jesus spoke these words he was physically in the world, therefore He could not live in the heart of His disciples. He was telling them that He would come to dwell in our midst, and that His presence **(parousia)** would live in our hearts.

He said to Paul when He appeared to him on the road to *Damascus* that He will appear to him many times in the same manner.

But rise and stand on your feet; for I have appeared to you for this purpose, to make you a minister and a witness both of the things which you have seen and of the things which I will yet reveal to you.   Acts 26:16

INSTRUMENT 4
THE SNATCHING AWAY THEORY
BY APOSTLE FERNANDO ORIHUELA

T he teaching about a secret coming before the manifestation of the man of sin has been much taught -and believed- only after the 19th century. The majority of Christians have accepted this with little or no research. Regardless of how impacting it may sound, this teaching was not the position of the early Church, or the reformers, or anybody's, until around the year 1830. The teaching about a secret rapture before the tribulation is not part of the original faith given to the saints.

After looking at Church history's big picture, Professor George Ladd stated, "All the Church fathers who write about this matter think the Church will suffer at the hands of the antichrist...we cannot find any trace of pre-tribulationism in the primitive church and not one of the modern pre-tribulationists have proved that this doctrine was believed in by any of the church fathers or by any of the students of the Word before the XIX century."[53]

Many accredited men of God stand out in Christian history: John

---
[53] George E. Ladd, The Blessed Hope (Grand Rapids: Eerdmans, 1956), p.31.

Wyclif, John Huss, Martin Lutero, Phillip Melanchton, Huldreich Zwinglio, William Tyndale, Nicholas Ridley, Hugh Latimer, John Fox, Edwin Sandys, John Calvin, John Knox, Isaac Newton and John Wesley; none of these men believed the Church would be removed before the manifestation of the antichrist. They believed that the Church would suffer at the hands of the antichrist, whose career would then end with Christ's coming.

What is now taught with great confidence is that the rapture will take away the saved to Heaven before the antichrist and before the coming of Christ in power and glory. What few people know is that this doctrine's origin is comparatively modern.

Edward Irving was born in *Scotland* in 1792. An eloquent preacher with a remarkable anointing, already in 1828 his open-air meetings attracted more than 10,000 people. Hundreds filled his church week after week. In 1832 he wrote a treatise that suggested Jesus had a fallen human nature. This caused such a great controversy amidst his congregation that he was removed from his pulpit. An ecclesiastical trial in 1833 took away his status as clergyman from the Church of Scotland and he passed away the following year in *Glasgow*.[54]

In September 1830, Irving's journal, *The Morning Watch*, published an article that introduced a two-phased idea regarding the coming of Christ. Many believe the seeds of this doctrine came from a Spanish book, *The Coming of Messiah in Glory and Majesty*, written by Manuel Lacunza – a priest and Chilean Jesuit theologian born in 1731 who proposed a millennialist interpretation of the

---

[54] LeRoy E. Froom, *The Prophetic faith of Our Fathers* (Washington: Review and Herald, 1945), Vol. 3, p. 516.

281

Catholic Bible prophecies,[55] which was translated into English by Irving in 1827.[56] This book, originally published in 1812, stated: '"when the Lord shall come from Heaven to Earth, upon His coming, and long before His arrival to Earth, shall give His command and send His mandates...with a shout...with the voice of the archangel and with the trump of God. Those who hear this voice of the Son of God shall resurrect right away."[57]

Shortly thereafter, the secret coming was taught among a group named the Plymouth Brethren, a movement composed of people who became disappointed with the sleepy condition that prevailed in many of the churches. This teaching was accepted by some and rejected by others. In 1864, S.P. Tregelles, one of the brethren who rejected this teaching wrote, "I was not aware of the existence of any definite teaching about a Church's secret rapture by a secret coming until this was introduced 'in a prophecy' in Mr. Irving's church which was perceived as the voice of the Spirit. But whether anybody was right about it or not, it arose from that alleged revelation along with a modern doctrine and modern phraseology. It came, not from the Holy Spirit but from one who feigned to be the Spirit of God."[58]

Curiously enough, this new revelation -the teaching about a separate coming to take away those who were ready- was to be

---

[55] http://es.wikipedia.org/wiki/Manuel_Lacunza, researched on September 2011.
John L. Bray, The Origin of the Pre-Tribulation Rapture Teaching (Lakeland, FL:

[56] John L. Bray, The Origin of the Pre-Tribulation Rapture Teaching (Lakeland, FL: John L. Bray Ministry, Inc., 1982).

[57] Manuel de Lacunza, The Coming of Messiah in Glory and Majesty (London: translated by Edward Irving, 1827), Vol 1, p. 99.

[58] S.P.Tregelles, The Hope of Christ's Second Coming (London: Samuel Bagster and Sons, 1864), pp.34-37.

dogmatically defended as if it had always been an eternal truth from Scripture. In the years to follow, this two-phased coming teaching was developed by John Nelson Darby (1800-1882). He became a leader among the Plymouth Brethren.

At the end, through the *Scoffield Bible,* many ended up believing in a secret rapture. Oswald J. Smith was one of them but later wrote, "Now after many years of studying and praying, I am absolutely convinced that there will be no taking away before the tribulation... I simply believed in another theory because I was taught by W.E. Blackstone's book *Jesus is Coming, Scoffield's Bible,* prophetic conferences and Bible schools, but when I began scrutinizing Scripture, I discovered that there was no verse that supported the pre-tribulation theory."[59]

Presently, this teaching is repeated by hundreds of ministers throughout the world without knowing its origin.

In the *Book of the Acts of the Apostles* one can read:

Repent ye therefore, and be converted, that your sins may be blotted out, when the times of refreshing shall come from the presence of the Lord.
And he shall send Jesus Christ, which before was preached unto you:
Whom the heaven must receive until the times of restitution of all things, which God hath spoken by the mouth of all his holy prophets since the world began.

Acts 3:19-21

---

[59] Smith, op.cit.,pp.2,3.

The word *restitution* in Greek is **apokatástasis.** This word comes from **apo** which means "in return", or "once again" and **katastemi,** which means "put in order."[60]

We are undeniably living in these times of restoration, since God is raising scholars and ministers who have the boldness to revisit subjects that are now the objects of new discussion. Certainly the eschatology issue is one that carries the most doubts, and yet is the least likely one that men want to tackle, simply because the price is too high. Many doors will close simply because the revelation-less Church has lost their capacity to reflect on the things they believe. Unfortunately, doctrinal tradition weighs so heavily that it goes above the principles of love and respect; many people could rupture their friendships with other ministers solely because they have changed their thinking about a doctrinal issue.

---

[60] *Strong's Concordance G605.*

I want to propose what appears to be the logical order to understand the *Book of Revelation.* As I previously stated, this is not a chronological book. The judgments and heavenly scenes are occurring simultaneously in God's timeless realm.

I also want to remind you that when the Canon was put together, the different parts of the *Book of Revelation* were not in order. Men were the ones who established its chapters and titles. Some of these have been placed according to their interpretation which compel compel the reader to a determinate interpretation. These titles do not form part of the Word revealed by God, nor do any titles in any Bibles.

This order is only a suggestion; it is by no means an imposition or an immovable truth.

Chapter 1: *The revelation of Jesus Christ*

Chapters 2 and 3: *The Message to the Seven Churches*

Chapter 19: *The New Jerusalem, Christ's Wife (21st in the Bible)*

Chapter 20: *The Description of the New Jerusalem continued until Verse 5 (22nd in the Bible)*

Chapter 21: *The Spiritual Kingdom that satan cannot touch. (20th in the Bible up to verse 10)*

Chapter 22: *The Final Judgment (20th in the Bible beginning with verse 11)*

Chapter 23: *The Angel and the Little Book and the Epilogue (10th and 22nd :6-21 in the Bible)*

Ana Méndez Ferrell, INC.

Visit our online store at

www.AnaMendezFerrell.com

Write to: Ana Méndez Ferrell, Inc.
P. O. Box 141
Ponte Vedra, FL 32004-0141
United States of America

Email: store@anamendezferrell.com

Like us on **FACEBOOK** or watch us on **YOUTUBE**

www.facebook.com/AnaMendezFerrellFanPage

www.youtube.com/Voiceofthelight